MORE GOOD JOBS

Peter

Building a cadre of Highly Influential People to support the cause is a winning strategy. Never give up - this is how we create More Good Jobs!

Martin

June 2021

MORE GOOD

JOBS

AN ENTREPRENEUR'S ACTION PLAN
TO CREATE CHANGE IN YOUR COMMUNITY

MARTIN BABINEC

LIONCREST
PUBLISHING

MORE GOOD JOBS

An Entrepreneur's Action Plan to Create Change in Your Community

ISBN   978-1-5445-0848-1 *Hardcover*
       978-1-5445-0846-7 *Paperback*
       978-1-5445-0847-4 *Ebook*

My soul mate, who always believed and supported, even in the darkest hours when these crazy ambitions were so hard to understand, much less embrace. Your conviction for me to stay the course, while keeping all in the family on board, made all the difference.

CONTENTS

FOREWORD

As an entrepreneur and venture capitalist, I've helped start, grow, and invest in emerging tech companies for over thirty years. Through these experiences, I've come to appreciate the critical role of a supportive local community in helping entrepreneurs and their startups beat the odds to succeed. And, in this success, I've seen the dramatic impact these entrepreneurs and the startups they create can have back on their local community over the long term.

I moved from Boston, Massachusetts, to Boulder, Colorado, at the end of 1995. This was a huge change for me and my wife, Amy Batchelor, from the startup-dense Boston area that was home for me since I showed up at MIT as a freshman 1983. When I showed up in Boulder a dozen years later, it had a tech community, but it wasn't a place you would find VCs hanging out looking for the next big thing.

Moving to Boulder caused me to look at community in a different way. Since I didn't know anyone, I began searching for other entrepreneurs who shared the passion I had for building companies. Along the way, I discovered and helped develop a connected community of entrepreneurs who worked together to build a vibrant startup community in Boulder.

This didn't happen quickly, but our small group kept growing and good things happened even though the macroeconomy had its ups and downs. Our efforts contributed to spawning and growing so many startups that a 2013 Kauffman Foundation report ranked Boulder as having the highest startup density in the entire United States.

Today, Boulder enjoys a strong economy on key measures such as total jobs, household income, diversity of industries, tax revenue collected, and contributions to public services and nonprofits. Growth in the Boulder startup community helped lead that change by harnessing many of the forces and approaches outlined in this book.

Martin Babinec shares my passion for helping others start and grow companies, proving it with contributions he has made across different initiatives since we first became friends in early 1990s while I was still living in Boston. Martin's track record building TriNet in Silicon Valley gives him both entrepreneurial street cred and a vantage point to grasp the needs and challenges of emerging tech entrepreneurs, especially since these types of companies were TriNet's customers throughout his twenty-year tenure as CEO.

Martin is one of the few people from outside Boulder who tracked what we were doing here from the beginning. From early on, he looked for ways to adapt that into what he was doing with his own efforts. His move from Silicon Valley back to his rural home of Upstate New York ignited his own passion for looking at the challenge of how to take what we know from the large entrepreneurial ecosystems like Silicon Valley and repurpose appropriate things to work in a totally different environment.

When he approached me in 2010 about his starting a non-profit with the goal of creating a connected startup community encompassing the entire Upstate New York region, I thought, "Who better than Martin to do in Upstate New York what I helped do in Boulder?" While I had plenty of data points from my experience in Boulder, I expected the challenge of connecting resources across multiple communities the size of a state would be more difficult. I hoped to learn from observing and correspondingly hoped my experience would be helpful to Martin.

With perseverance, lots of experiments, and plenty of adaptation, the Upstate New York entrepreneurial ecosystem is now evolving with a growing community engagement that you will see profiled in this book. This was made possible by the simple premise of starting with a small group of like-minded people who banded together with a shared vision and set of principles. These leaders committed for the long haul, knowing it would take many years to bring about the cultural change needed for community transformation.

This book presents a diverse menu of approaches community leaders can pick from. The choices are born out of real-life experience that rings true from my viewpoint as a participant and observer of entrepreneurial ecosystem-building around the globe.

While *More Good Jobs* includes excerpts of the Boulder story and Techstars, I found many fresh, new insights. Martin's book is a great resource for leaders who are looking to jump in and start transforming their local community. I've learned a lot and hope you will also.

Brad Feld
Co-founder, Foundry Group
Co-founder, Techstars
Boulder, CO
May 2020

INTRODUCTION

I am the product of two valleys.

I was born and raised in Upstate New York's Mohawk Valley. As many in my area do, after college I left to pursue my dreams elsewhere. Unlike many others, I ended up boomeranging back home twenty-five years later.

The Mohawk Valley is placed within a larger region that is an undisputed talent factory, attracting students globally to attend our world-renowned colleges and universities. New York has more students traveling in from other areas to attend college than any other state.[1] As a whole, the one-hundred-plus Upstate colleges enroll almost a half-million students, including tens of thousands of STEM students, making it one of the largest STEM cohorts of any geographic region in the country.

There's a flip side: we wave goodbye to far too many of our next generation leaving Upstate New York after graduating college as they search for better opportunities elsewhere.

---

[1]   The Commission on Independent Colleges and Universities in New York, "CICU Fact Sheet 2019–20," CICU, April 2020, http://cicu.org/application/files/8115/7252/9390/CICU_Fact_Sheet_2019-20.pdf.

Silicon Valley is my other world, the place where I landed in the late 1980s due to my job transfer. I arrived with no advance plan or relationships, and after two years of a frustrating search for a new job, I decided to leave my setting of secure employment to start what I hoped would become a successful small business in the then-unheard-of category of human resource outsourcing.

What followed was a roller-coaster story of Silicon Valley challenge and opportunity. A ride that I am still on today as a board member of my company, TriNet, a New York Stock Exchange–traded company with annual revenues of about $4 billion.

In the twenty years I served as TriNet's founding CEO, our principal target market was emerging technology companies and supporting ecosystem players who invested in or served these high-growth organizations. Since TriNet provides the full range of human capital management to help these firms grow, I had an insider's view into how innovation economy companies get started and grow, initially in Silicon Valley and, over time, in all the major tech innovation hubs in the United States.

I first began to pay attention to the contrast between my two valleys as my wife and I traveled back home with our children to visit our extended families. Over a decade of these trips, our priorities evolved around the setting we felt would be best for raising our three children. It was during the summer of 1999—while TriNet was on the cusp of seeking an initial public offering (IPO) at the very height of the dot-com boom—that we made the life-altering decision to relocate back to my hometown of Little Falls, New York.

The plan was for me to cross-country commute for eighteen to twenty-four months before passing the CEO baton to another person. But the dot-com collapse thwarted that scenario. Tri-Net's planned IPO was aborted post roadshow on pricing day, in October 2000, and my commute ground on for a full ten years as we rebuilt the company following a painful series of layoffs.

Living a bicoastal existence with long commute times (and no direct flights from Upstate to the West Coast!) spurred lots of reflection on the contrasts between my two valleys. It was over this decade, commuting between these two worlds, that I observed the stark reality of the similarities and differences between them.

Both regions produced incredible numbers of talented young people. And yet Silicon Valley was thriving with a magnetic pull for retaining and attracting these young people from elsewhere, while my Mohawk Valley seemed to be moving backward by exporting them.

Logging more than a million miles in cross-country flights during this period prompted lots of reflection on why this gap was so vast, even when discounted for obvious differences of population density and current industry clusters. The business community across Upstate New York seemed to be rallying against the high taxes and unfriendly business regulations, claiming that smaller government would fix our problems. But as I looked around the country, this didn't feel right. California certainly wasn't known for its business-friendly regulation or low taxes. Neither was Boston or New York City. It seemed there needed to be a better reason for this divide I was experiencing.

I thought back to my own experience. What if I had decided to start TriNet while living someplace other than the San Francisco Bay Area? How would it have turned out? Did we owe some portion of our company's success to the unique environment that Silicon Valley had to offer?

HOW SILICON VALLEY SAVED TRINET

About four years into the commute, we righted the TriNet ship and were sailing fast back into high growth waters. The company's value was reestablished to the point that I knew I would not have to worry about having to take another job to fulfill our family's financial needs.

As I thought through all the steps of the entrepreneurial journey that led to that financial freedom, my "aha!" was realizing that had I attempted to start TriNet in Upstate New York, I would have failed. Same guy, same idea, same starting knowledge and capital position—just a different location—and there was no doubt in my mind that the business wouldn't have succeeded.

I could pinpoint at least one pivotal moment in our journey where Silicon Valley's culture directly saved our company. About a year after starting TriNet, we'd fallen so far behind our original growth projections that the realities were starting to settle in. My startup optimism was quickly fading into a gloomier picture about whether small business owners would see value in outsourcing their human resources function to us. Even with just a small team, minimal overhead, and my working without a salary, we were hemorrhaging cash and rapidly using up whatever I could borrow from friends and family.

Out of desperation to avoid closure, I reimagined our entire marketing approach to shift away from the traditional small business customers we had been trying to sell, to instead focus exclusively on emerging tech companies, who were a better fit for the value proposition we offered. That shift in focus brought TriNet into the world of Silicon Valley, presenting a path a few brave angel investors believed in enough to support us with raising a total of $50,000 in equity capital.

This manna from heaven not only staved off bankruptcy, but began the series of moves that would lead to TriNet's rise by being a niche market player dedicated to the emerging tech community. Looking at the path along which this rise unfolded—leveraging proximity to tech startups and innovation economy companies, the openness of the Silicon Valley community, and the attainable connections to mentors and investors—it was clear that none of this would have unfolded in my home area of Upstate New York, or many other areas of the country at that time.

My success was, thus, a byproduct of having been lucky enough to be in Silicon Valley when starting my first company. I was the beneficiary of having been in the most entrepreneur-supportive place on the planet at TriNet's most formative stage.

TO WHOM MUCH HAS BEEN GIVEN...

With financial independence and that critical realization of how important a supportive ecosystem is, I began to think more about what I could do to play a role in creating this environment for others. I wasn't satisfied with being limited to just those entrepreneurs I could help individually. Instead, I wanted to tackle the much larger challenge of bringing about a shift in the direction of an entire regional economy—a goal most everyone would quickly say was unattainable.

But that's what we as entrepreneurs do. When we see a gap between current reality and what we believe is possible, we don't get stopped by prevailing views on why something can't be done. Instead we ask, why not? If not now, when? If not me, who?

So, after stepping down as TriNet chairman at the start of 2010, I began my transition into work on this journey, beginning with the launch of Upstate Venture Connect, a nonprofit with the mission of building a region-wide startup community that connects high-growth founders with the people and resources needed for success. I'm still working full throttle on that today: understanding the forces at work behind the loss of a region's best talent, and creating a roadmap to engage others in banding together so we can collectively sow seeds for restoring economic vitality.

TALENT FLIGHT FROM HOLLOWING CITIES

In the 1970s, Upstate New York had over 1.5 million manufacturing jobs.[2] Most of the top employers were unionized factories paying high enough wages for a single income to support a middle-class family, just as my dad did for his family with seven children.

Surrounding those factories were local suppliers, builders, restaurants, and other private and public services that were all part of an ecosystem supporting manufacturing. Success in the industrial era is what powered building Upstate's terrific infrastructure, great arts and recreation, and also that extensive network of colleges and universities.

---

2   US Department of Labor.

In our area, and many others throughout middle America, over the last fifty years we've seen a steady erosion of those manufacturing jobs that has hollowed out once proud and strong communities. As a result, we are dealing with growing poverty, underemployment, stagnant wages, urban and rural decay, drug abuse, and a loss of the hope and optimism for a promising future that my parents' generation enjoyed.

While there remains a service economy involving schools, healthcare, nonprofits, retail, and agriculture, what is lacking in my region are growth opportunities in expanding industries that capture the interest and passion of the next generation.

As a result, too many recent grads are leaving. A recent report by the Pew Research Center followed graduates on F-1 visas to observe where they relocated within the United States after their education. Buffalo suffered the biggest outflow of graduates, with only 25 percent remaining after their degree. Other Upstate cities like Syracuse and Rochester weren't far behind.[3] Where did they go? Across these three university metro areas, the Pew data says out-migration went to the same top four destinations: New York City, the San Francisco Bay Area, Boston, and the Northern Virginia / DC metroplex.

Young people implicitly understand that living in a region with more good jobs means more income, more opportunities, more interesting people, and a more vibrant culture. It's natural for the next generation, with promising ambition and few ties, to move to where they perceive these opportunities to be.

---

3   The data on this trend tracks foreign students, and unfortunately there is no comparable dataset for US citizens. I believe this is a fruitful area for further research: https://www.pewresearch.org/global/interactives/where-do-foreign-student-graduates-work-in-the-united-states/.

The hundreds of millions of Americans making similar decisions have impacted our social fabric. Families are being needlessly separated—dividing parents from their children and grandparents from their grandchildren—because we aren't able to create the excitement and opportunities in our hometowns that exist in larger innovation hubs.

Joel Giambra, a 2018 gubernatorial candidate here in New York, summed up the view instantly grasped by parents, grandparents, uncles, aunts, and so many others who watch our next generation of talent departing when he described the Buffalo airport as "the runway of tears."

HOW TO SOLVE THE PROBLEM

When faced with the stark reality of our struggling cities, too many of us instinctively turn to government to solve our problems. The macroeconomic changes we need, it seems, can only happen from the top down, and if we want to shift the trend back toward the forgotten areas in our country, we somehow think politicians should be the ones to drive change to make it happen.

Political leaders with a conservative bent typically fall back on the mantra of lower taxes and less government being what's needed to turn the economy around, but somehow they all seem to be overlooking that most of the very cities producing the greatest amount of innovation and high-paying job growth are also the ones with high taxes and burdensome government.

Other leaders (both liberal and conservative) propose solutions including tax abatement packages and other forms of mild bribery aimed at bringing large corporations to weaker economies. These attempts are well-intentioned, but as we'll show in subsequent chapters, the incentives don't deliver on job creation goals announced at launch and are usually a mistake in hindsight. Tax abatement packages, at their core, are subsidies by the rest of us to help pad profits for a business that doesn't really need it.

These strategies have not proven their ability to create more good jobs at a cost that makes sense to taxpayers. When we look at the places where true, organic creation of good jobs has happened, it hasn't been fueled by top-down policies or tax incentives. The best talent flocking from our region to the San Francisco Bay Area, New York City, Boston, and Northern Virginia / DC aren't deterred from starting companies in those locations by their high taxes and more burdensome government or lured there by some government programs.

Having lived the life of two valleys, I can say with conviction that the difference between growth and decline isn't government policy or regional planning but instead how each area evolved with regards to *whether the community embraces or ignores innovators that actually create companies and jobs.*

NOW IS THE TIME

Changing a city's culture may seem like a daunting task, but it's a problem I've been studying since those cross-country flights over a decade ago. After exploring what's behind the country's most innovative cities, I've come to my own understanding of the patterns that allow these innovation hubs to flourish and have experimented for the last decade on implementing strategies empowering change in my own region.

This book captures some findings from that work. I'm not an economist or researcher, though I've gotten help from people with those skills. You'll see lots of examples of observations I've made or personally experienced in cities that either attract or export talent.

The research and writing was pretty much completed when the COVID-19 pandemic swept through the United States, shuttering businesses and driving unemployment to levels none thought even remotely possible during the boom period running right up until early March 2020.

So, even though we aren't through the resolution to this pandemic as this book goes to print, we anticipate some cascading changes ahead. Individuals may reset their life priorities, migration may flow from the densest urban areas to rural regions, and significant unemployment levels may sweep across broad sectors of the US economy. These and other forces will put pressures on policy makers and community leaders to act decisively in responding to an increasing demand for growing more jobs, perhaps opening up receptivity to new approaches we'll describe in these pages.

With this book, it's my hope to find those leaders in other communities who might be interested in bringing about change in the lives of those around us. To do so, we need to be both informed about forces and patterns not well documented in today's media and also equipped with specific strategies that can be iterated for adopting in our community or region. Creating more jobs—more good jobs—is within our reach.

Sadly, a goal this big discourages some people from considering it. We think that to have an impact, we need to change everything all at once. But that isn't the case.

Individuals, especially entrepreneurs, have the ability to meaningfully contribute toward transforming our communities as long as we're ready to make a long-term commitment.

Bringing about change is an incremental process, accomplished one step at a time. It doesn't need to be a full-time job for someone to make a meaningful contribution. Building a thriving, innovative community only requires a handful of people who are intentional about the culture they are trying to create and ready to seek out collaboration opportunities with other like-minded people who are ready to start making things happen.

Leading change also shouldn't be relegated to being a big, lofty goal to take on when we retire from our businesses or professional roles. This is a goal to start working toward today. If there's one thing I've seen while working with thousands of entrepreneurs over the years, it's that so many of them want to give back. We love to build things, improve the world, and make people's lives better.

Unfortunately, too many entrepreneurs wait until later in our journey to begin channeling our talents to causes beyond our own companies. The intense focus required in creating and growing a company is certainly one reason for this. But even while growing the company, there are a range of choices that could be beneficial to both our business and our community if we open up consideration beyond the bubble of our immediate company needs.

Another obstacle to entrepreneurs giving back can be frustration around how ineffective our options look to have the social impact we seek.

If we've exited a company, maybe we look at sitting on one or more nonprofit boards but can't handle the bureaucracy. Or we think about advocating policy or running for public office, but the pace and polarization of politics drives us crazy. Yes, we want to make sustainable, lasting change for many people, but we don't know how to do it, so we go back to the familiar by just starting another company.

With the strategies described in this book, I hope to share realistic paths on how we might nudge positive change toward community job creation *while* still engaged in running a business or organization—and in a way that feels sustainable and substantial.

We, as individuals, can make a real impact in our community, creating a culture of innovation, helping new entrepreneurs succeed, and creating more good jobs. Our potential impact is massive, and we already have the ability to do it. This book will show you how.

I promise, you have a fun and rewarding journey ahead. Let's get started.

PART 1

UNDERSTANDING THE PROBLEM

CHAPTER 1

WHAT ARE INNOVATION ECONOMY JOBS AND WHY DO WE WANT MORE OF THEM?

To be what we are, and to become what we are capable of becoming, is the only end of life.
—ROBERT LOUIS STEVENSON

In today's sound-bite driven news world, it's hard to go five minutes without hearing someone sharing their perspective on jobs: *We need lower unemployment! Higher wages! Better job training! Bring back jobs from overseas!*

For better or for worse, jobs are the center around which the modern world turns. Through the income we receive, jobs provide the means to support our needs and wants, and in many cases, also bring a sense of purpose to our lives.

Beyond the impact on our own lives and families, the income we earn and then spend locally is a factor in creating jobs for others in the community. Individuals and businesses earning more income creates more local spending, feeding the creation of more jobs in other companies as a result.

The economy—and to some extent, the world—is a tangled network of jobs. From firefighters to office workers to entrepreneurs, we are all doing our part to support the wants and needs of the rest of humanity and, in exchange, we receive income to support our own wants and needs (which we accomplish by paying others to do their jobs).

When this cycle is flowing, everyone wins. In a Utopian world, we would each find meaningful work that matters to us, use it as a vehicle to serve others, and earn an income in the process. But the reality is rarely this rosy. In today's world, much of the conversation about jobs is focused on what happens when there isn't enough good work to go around. Communities without good work prospects shrink as people vote with their feet by moving elsewhere. Soon, the Utopian cycle has reversed itself, with a lack of work resulting in a lack of both income and wealth generation needed to create more good jobs, which further exacerbates the problem.

WHAT IS A GOOD JOB?

To keep our communities strong, we need to create more good jobs—jobs that people want and will stick around for. Much of this book will focus on what we can do to accomplish this, but before we get there, it is worth pausing to discuss what, exactly, we mean by good jobs.

All jobs aren't created equal, but defining what exactly makes a good job isn't as straightforward as it seems. For example, is the job of a big-time lawyer better than that of a passionate but poorly paid artist? Only the individual can make that decision.

So what makes a job good in the first place? We can look at this from three perspectives:

First, the better a job is, the better it has to be for the person working it. Paying more, providing better benefits, and stimulating them in a way that challenges and fulfills them with purpose are all ways in which jobs accomplish this. To put this simply, jobs that individuals want are better than jobs that someone might endure but doesn't really want.

Second, the better a job is, the better it is for the company doing the hiring. Good jobs attract the best talent, which is a win for the company—having the best talent can power the business ahead of their competitors. As with any company investment, the cost of filling the job has to be offset by the person filling the job delivering enough value for the business's customers to pay for. In other words, jobs that cost more for the company to fill reflect the higher value that these jobs have in being tied to the success of the company.

Lastly, the better a job is, the better it is for the wider community. Good jobs should raise up the community, making it a better place for others to live and work. That means contributing productively to the community, and, as we'll see, bringing more wealth into the community to create jobs for others.

But creating jobs isn't something we can just do overnight. No one has a magic wand to make jobs appear. Private-sector jobs are only created when a company has a specific need that warrants making the investment to pay for someone filling the job. No matter how much a community might want more good jobs, it's the basic market forces of the demand for a company's product or service that will end up driving the actual rate of growing job volume and quality.

There is, however, one path into job creation behind many of the country's fastest growing job markets that has evolved without being directed by government policy or taxpayer resources.

From Silicon Valley and New York City to smaller metros like Boulder, Colorado, and Austin, Texas, communities have benefited from growing large numbers of what I call innovation economy jobs. These jobs not only meet the above criteria of being better for the person, the company, and the community, but they are also the key to larger demographic changes that can power a city's overall growth in other jobs, wages, and wealth.

And, luckily for us, there are changes going on that leaders of communities everywhere can tap into to kick-start the creation of innovation economy jobs, no matter where their community is located.

Before we dive into how to create more innovation economy jobs, let's establish what they are and why they are so important.

First, a definition: I'll refer to an innovation economy company as "a business whose product or service is based on an innovation not yet widely adopted, but with the intent of growing toward a national or global audience."

To be clear, that innovation doesn't need to be limited to developing new technology, since new products and services arise out of mixing up components of things already around us to offer something few of us have ever seen before.

It also doesn't require being the first to market. When we refer to innovation, we mean that the company is providing an innovative solution that addresses a market need, not necessarily that the company is creating a major technological breakthrough.

The second half of the definition—the focus on a national or global audience—is crucially important. As we will see throughout the rest of this chapter, deploying an offering to a larger audience beyond local customers is a key driver of job creation that results from innovation economy companies.

WHY ARE INNOVATION ECONOMY COMPANIES CREATING THE MOST GOOD JOBS?

When we begin to compare innovation economy jobs to the criteria of a good job defined above, the first factor to consider is that they are good for the people who work in them.

Because these companies are based on creating and bringing an innovation to market, they require a type of talent that isn't in great supply. It takes a special kind of person to help create and rapidly iterate something new that others will buy.

The high demand is based on the enormous growth potential of these industries, and the low supply of skilled, adaptable people who can fill the roles, leads to exceptionally high wages. That may seem basic or obvious, but it's important to remember: these high wages aren't an accident—it's a signal there is a shortage of people who can fill these unusually demanding roles.

Companies that employ workers in innovation economy jobs tend to treat their employees better, as it is the only way they'll be successful in attracting and keeping this in-demand talent.

We can see evidence of this not only with the high wages paid, but also in the perks and benefits at these companies: very flexible time-off policies, an incredible array of medical and insurance benefits, company contributions to 401(k) plans, and some workplaces with free food and on-site personal services.

Beyond basic workplace benefits, it is most typically innovation economy companies that offer wealth-building potential through the company's sharing of equity in the form of stock options or grants—not just to executives, but to large segments of the company's workforce.

TriNet has helped tens of thousands of innovation economy companies over the last thirty years, so I can say from experience that beyond high wages and rich benefits, these companies strive to do everything they can to serve their employees, as it's an imperative for them to retain the very best talent.

The demand for innovation economy talent is so great that if the employees don't feel they are working in the right place, they have a much easier time finding the next job than employees in stable or shrinking industries. This puts pressure on the innovation economy company to offer the right kind of work environment that both attracts and keeps the best talent.

Innovation economy jobs tend to be in burgeoning industries, with high levels of private investment attracted by the potential for big payoffs for success. Companies that find traction with investors and customers can be sufficiently capitalized to pay higher salaries and offer employees growth opportunities from very early stages of their company life cycle. These aren't dying industries trying to squeeze the most out of their limited assets—they take risks toward achieving the vision of becoming giants of the future, attractive to investors and employees alike.

In the industrial age, companies derived their value from the enormous amounts of capital-intensive physical plant, machinery, and sales and marketing muscle needed to bring a product to market. Today's innovation economy companies know that their greatest assets aren't physical buildings and machinery, but instead the talent that walks out the door every night. If they are to succeed in the competitive world of constant innovation, they have to retain that talent by not just having high wages, but also demonstrating all the attributes of being a good employer. This seeming burden on the employer is actually worthwhile, because the innovation economy jobs serve both the company's and employee's best interests.

All of these companies that are based on human talent and ingenuity—rather than equipment or capital—are made possible by the existence of the innovation economy. In what other era could a group of thirteen people get together, work from their laptops to design and code software, and end up selling their product, Instagram, for $1 billion only eighteen months later? The amount of value that can be created by people in innovation economy jobs supported with minimal capital investments over such a short time period outweighs anything we've seen in the history of mankind.

In addition to simply creating more value for the companies where they work, people in innovation economy jobs tend to attract more people like them, which helps other companies in the community thrive. Economists refer to this as the agglomeration principle, and we'll go into greater detail as we discuss the cyclical nature of innovation economy jobs.

At its core, the agglomeration principle we're applying here is simple: *the more people who enter a community that is expanding the number of innovation economy jobs, the more who will end up following them.*

This is helpful to both employees and employers in a region's innovation economy. Picking up and moving across the country for a new opportunity can be a scary thing, but it's made easier for workers when they know they are entering a thriving community full of good jobs.

Without this community, many recruits pondering relocation worry: *Will I enjoy living in this new city? Will I be able to find friends who are like me? Will my spouse/partner be able to find a job? If things don't work out at my new company, will I be able to find another opportunity without having to relocate a second time?*

This is true in other industries as well. For example, *Outside* magazine, based in New Mexico, can face difficulty hiring editors from New York, and Virgin Galactic, building rocket ships in the desert, can struggle to attract talent to their remote location. In many ways, this is why cities exist: to bring together opportunities and people in a way that makes relocating a less risky proposition.

As more and more talented workers enter the local workforce, companies stand to benefit once again. In industries where growth is limited by talent, a growing workforce of talented people able to work in today's newer industries is a key advantage. As more jobs are created in these newer industries, companies are given the gift of a stronger talent base to pick from. If you're in one of these newer industries that's based on the intellectual capital that you need to be successful, you can no longer operate in the mindset that you're going to keep your employees captive at your company. They can and will leave, starting their own companies or chasing other opportunities—which can all be good things for adding to the community's job growth.

Lastly, but arguably most importantly, innovation economy jobs are simply more valuable for the community than any other category of jobs. Whether you are a retiree living in a community or a low-skilled worker entering the workforce earning minimum wage, as we'll show in upcoming chapters, an influx of innovation economy jobs in a community powers both more jobs in other categories and also a rise in wages that brings benefit to raising the overall quality of life in the community.

HISTORICAL FORCES THAT HAVE SHAPED JOB CREATION

To appreciate the significance of the job-generating impact of innovation economy jobs, it's helpful to first think about the historical connection between how productive an individual worker's output is to the growth of jobs and rising wages.

If we look back to the job market of the eighteenth century, the majority of US jobs were rooted in agriculture. Over the nineteenth century, we saw the gradual rise of jobs in industrial settings as factories began producing goods for consumers, other businesses, and government. An individual working in a factory could contribute a higher amount of economic value (more dollars of revenue for the company) than that same individual could produce working on a farm.

This permitted factory owners to pay higher wages to that worker than the farm owner could, starting with Henry Ford's famous five-dollar day rate in the early 1900s. As more and more of these high-wage opportunities for factory employment came about, so did the migration of labor from the farm to the factory.

Productivity gains created by new categories of jobs with high output of value per worker are trends to watch not only for common elements that are underlying drivers behind the creation of those jobs, but also for the impact of rising wages in the new high-productivity jobs and *ancillary jobs that might be created around them.*

While the concept of some jobs having a multiplier effect in creating other jobs is not new, economist Enrico Moretti's research in his groundbreaking 2012 book, *The New Geography of Jobs,* put a spotlight on how innovation economy jobs have the greatest job multiplier effect of all.

Put simply, the multiplier effect is the idea that when a member of a community earns a salary, that money isn't something that's used up and disappears. Instead, some portion of the salary is spent in the community, which creates other jobs for members of the community, who then spend a portion of their salary locally, which fuels creation of even more jobs in the community.

Moretti's research showed that different types of work create different job creation multipliers.

For example, local service work has a very low job multiplier because the productivity of these jobs remains largely flat, since the jobs haven't benefited as much from advances in technology and global logistics as jobs in other sectors have. Think about the work of fitness instructors, landscapers, restaurant workers, physicians, attorneys, or other local service providers. While they all benefit in some fashion by having access to certain tools or information made possible by technology development, the work itself requires similar amounts of labor as it has in the past.

In contrast, throughout much of the twentieth century, manufacturing work was the economic engine for a broad base of both rural and urban communities because of its higher job multiplier. Moretti's research shows that for each manufacturing job, an additional 1.6 jobs were created in the local community. Manufacturing achieves this higher job multiplier from the confluence of several factors.

- Economic value of the output per worker is higher in manufacturing than in most production-level service jobs.
- Manufactured products are sold outside the local community (either nationally or globally), which has potential for larger scale and an influx of new money from outside the community.
- Supporting services, like key suppliers, could locate nearby the manufacturer, creating their own jobs that are tied to the manufacturer's business.
- Because productivity is higher, manufacturers typically pay higher wages than local service jobs, which leads to more disposable income to be spent locally on goods and services, which produces more jobs.
- With gains made through collective bargaining, manufacturing jobs are more likely than service jobs to provide

benefits and retirement plans, which keep residents spending even after they leave the job.

- As with any successful business, owners take profits out of the business and may even sell the company, which creates wealth that can be reinvested into the community through real estate development, donations to nonprofits, or starting or investing in new companies.

With these factors fueling the 1.6 to 1 job multiplier and foundation for a local economy, it's no wonder that our politicians and media are constantly harping about the need for more manufacturing as the key to stimulating job growth in local communities.

The problem is that the manufacturing workforce of a traditional manufacturing plant is mostly made up of low-skilled workers who can be trained to perform repetitive tasks in a reasonable time period.

As companies continuously work to reduce their costs, manufacturers gravitate toward relocating their plants to areas where costs like labor, energy, and taxes are lower. If a better deal can be found elsewhere, the typical assembly-line job can be filled by new workers in the more favorable environment, as long as the deal comes with enough benefit to offset the cost of relocation. As a result, much of the manufacturing industry is moving to lower-cost and regulatory-friendly settings, including outside the United States.

As will be explained in more depth in a later chapter on government, this "seek out the best deal" scenario then drives another set of issues, as politicians give away billions of our tax dollars to big corporations to relocate manufacturing plants in the name of economic development (or, more accurately, for the chance to get a ribbon-cutting photo op as part of their next election campaign).

MANUFACTURING IS NO LONGER THE BEST JOB CREATOR

While manufacturing will always have a significant place in the US economy, globalization and rapid advances in technology supporting the supply chain combine to drive a natural flow of factory jobs from high- to lower-cost areas and countries.

This doesn't mean there won't be any manufacturing jobs. Supply chain issues highlighting dependency on offshore manufacturing for essential drugs and personal protective equipment during the 2020 pandemic will undoubtedly put public policy and resources in the reshoring direction. Pre-pandemic, we were already underway with a renaissance of advanced manufacturing, featuring shorter production runs and rapid retooling for a more automated assembly line guided by highly skilled production workers. But these roles will be fewer in number than traditional manufacturing jobs, as their existence is premised on the advanced manufacturing factory being more labor-efficient than the lower-wage, lower-skilled option still available through relocation to a lower-cost environment.

The actual job data on what's happening in manufacturing employment is pretty sobering. As recently as 1985, US manufacturing totaled more than twenty million jobs. As of December 2017, US manufacturing was down to 12.5 million jobs.[4] Even with all the talk of recent changes in the political

---

4   Erin Duffin, "Number of private sector manufacturing employees in the United States from 1985 to 2019," *Statista*, March 17, 2020, https://www.statista.com/statistics/664993/ private-sector-manufacturing-employment-in-the-us/.

environment to stoke new US manufacturing jobs, continued erosion of traditional manufacturing prompts most economic forecasts to show little to no overall growth in the manufacturing sector.

Despite the reduction in the number of manufacturing jobs, with their 1.6 to 1 job multiplier, there is a compelling alternative model that can keep our local economies growing: innovation economy jobs. Companies in the innovation economy share a number of the factors that lead them to create a much higher job multiplier than manufacturing.

- The nature of the work performed inside an innovation economy company can often include extremely high economic value per worker.
- Innovation economy products and services are easily sold outside the local community through the internet, which creates potential for a larger scale and an influx of new money to the community where the company is based.
- Supporting services in the local area (e.g., consultants, property management, accountants, and other professionals) receive additional business, creating their own jobs that are tied to the innovation economy company's business.
- Innovation economy companies typically pay extremely high wages (much higher than manufacturing), which lead to more disposable income to be spent locally on goods and services, which produces more jobs. At the time I transitioned out of TriNet's CEO role in 2008, our innovation economy customers were paying average wages per employee of about $100,000 per year.
- Innovation economy jobs are more likely than service jobs to provide benefits and retirement plans, which keep residents spending locally even after they leave the job.

- Innovation economy companies can be investable, profitable, and sellable! Their owners take profits out of the business and/or sell the company, which then creates wealth that is reinvested into the community through real estate development, donations to nonprofits, or investing in and starting new companies. As will be detailed in subsequent chapters, this last factor is far more likely to propel job growth than any other industry, including the fact that many startups get sold for millions of dollars before they've ever reached their first dollar of profitability!

As you can see, innovation economy companies seem to have even more favorable customer geographies, more supporting services, higher wages, more benefits, and more wealth generated than manufacturing businesses. They also have a number of characteristics that the manufacturing industry doesn't have. For example, barriers to entry for creating an innovation economy company are historically low. Compared to manufacturing, which requires immense amounts of capital, professional websites can be created in an hour or less with off-the-shelf tools, low-cost cloud hosting, and on-demand software applications.

As a result, Moretti's research showed that for every one job created at an innovation economy company, five other jobs are created in the local economy. That 5 to 1 job multiplier is triple that of the manufacturing industry!

This isn't rocket science. Innovation economy companies provide high salaries, which lead to more discretionary income. People with high income contract out for more personal services, things like dog watching, childcare, dry cleaning, and going out to eat at restaurants. In other words, these people earn their money by doing work for a company with an offering aimed at a national or global scale, but disproportionately spend it locally, which leads to an influx of money flowing through the local economy.

The companies themselves also spend money in the local economy. Whether they are bootstrapped or funded by outside investors, innovation economy companies are under pressure to develop and get their product to market quickly. One way to keep their expensive talent focused on critical near-term priorities is to contract out noncore functions like design, accounting, HR, and facilities, thereby stoking job creation for local service providers of many flavors.

Whether it's hiring local marketing firms, lawyers, accountants, consultants, or maintenance workers, the companies follow a similar pattern to the employees—earning their money nationally or globally, and disproportionately spending it locally, supporting local services.

Not only do innovation economy jobs create wealth that flows through the local economy to lower-skilled jobs, they also give the people in those jobs opportunities to find higher-paying professions in newer industries.

For example, over TriNet's first ten to fifteen years in business, many of us would stop at Sabino's, our favorite coffee shop, on the way to the office. As our growth ramped up and we were hungry to hire more customer service people of our own, we plucked several right from our interactions at Sabino's—baristas who impressed us with their service ethic, as well as referrals to other local talent we got from friends in the shop.

Moving from part-time lower-skilled roles into TriNet became a transformative career move for many people. Not only because of the higher starting wages and full benefits, but also through their career growth, with many levels of opportunity that they simply would not have had in the local coffee shop. A community with an abundance of innovation economy companies looking to fill entry-level roles increases the ability of lower-skilled workers to find better employment opportunities.

RESEARCH BEHIND *MORE GOOD JOBS*

In writing this book, we were supported by a research team led by Professors Jason Kuruzovich of Rensselaer Polytechnic Institute and Brett Orzechowski of Utica College. Our project started with looking at some of the Moretti findings through data sources that could include communities outside the well-known tech hubs that get all the media attention.

In addition to looking at the job multiplier, which Moretti has already done a phenomenal job with, we sought to increase the scope of our analysis to investigate whether innovation economy jobs lead to other positive outcomes for the community.

We did this by analyzing data from Crunchbase, a platform for innovation economy companies that contains employee profiles for innovation economy workers. To ensure the data was consistent and accurate, we gathered all data from the years 2010–2017, for every city with a population between 1–2 million.

From this dataset, we were able to not only extract the locations of those working in innovation economy jobs, but also infer their previous location based on where they went to college. By cross-referencing this data with publicly available economic and labor force data about those cities, we were able to gain insight into the impact of talent migration on fueling growth of innovation economy jobs in a given community.

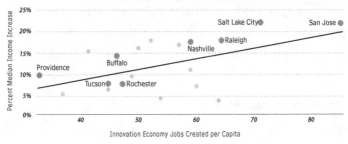

Innovation Economy Job Creation vs. Median Household Income Increase

Source: U.S. Census Bureau, Center for Economic Studies, LEHD

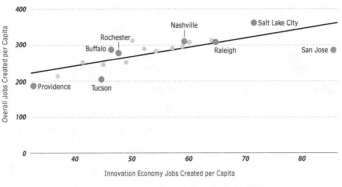

Innovation Economy Job Creation vs. Overall Job Creation

Source: U.S. Census Bureau, Center for Economic Studies, LEHD

The results were conclusive. Our research found that communities that created more innovation economy jobs correlated not only with increased overall job growth in the region, but also with increased median income across all sectors. In addition to research highlights mentioned in the book, we'll share other findings as well as back up data on our website, MoreGoodJobs.org.

In these charts, we can see cities like San Jose, Salt Lake City, Nashville, and Raleigh topping the list with the highest innovation economy job growth, and the corresponding increase in overall job growth and median income. On the other end of the spectrum, we see cities like Tucson, Buffalo, Rochester, and Providence with very low innovation economy job growth, and the negatives that come along with this. In the next chapter, we'll explore more of the why behind these gaps and start to discuss what we can do about it.

Beyond more job opportunities, companies that create higher wages benefit the community in other ways. As a simple example, more earnings lead to higher-priced home purchases that in turn increase local taxes for schools and city services shared by all families, regardless of earnings.

Increased wealth in the community also benefits nonprofits that can play a crucial role in helping to address needs not satisfied by government programs. Living in Upstate New York, I've seen firsthand what happens when nonprofits whose donors came from the once-thriving manufacturing industry are now starved for the dollars they need to stay afloat. The nonprofit community understands that it must get behind the creation of the next donor class. New wealth generation is crucial to keeping this part of the community strong and healthy, and delivering impact across areas like education, human services, the arts, and segments of society most in need.

We have heard people advocate that the positive cycle of attracting creative class talent actually begins by a community investing in public transportation, arts, recreation, and other community amenities that have a cumulative effect on quality of life. But I haven't seen the empirical evidence yet that access to amenities itself is responsible for driving job creation. I would be among those positing that quality arts, culinary options, entertainment, and recreation are more likely to grow as the result of job growth success and wealth generation in the community, and are not the drivers creating job growth in the first place.

You can see this by observing that some of the very large and once-booming cities, like Detroit, Cleveland, and Buffalo—all of whom still retain a vibrant arts and culture scene—have shrunk to become shells of their earlier success among the largest cities in the country.

One can also look at cities, like Berlin, that have invested phenomenally in the arts and created incredible cultures that appeal to today's mobile millennials in Europe. But without the connective tissue needed in the newer industries, there is lagging growth in innovation economy jobs needed to attract the critical mass of high performers who had options to go anywhere with their in-demand talent.

This makes logical sense. Although the arts are a major factor in whether people enjoy living in a city, the primary reason that talented young people move is for career opportunities. According to a recent survey by Indeed, 45 percent of Americans who relocate do so for career reasons.[5] It is true that arts and innovation economy jobs tend to go together, but I believe this correlation is due to the fact that more wealth in a city tends to lead to more investment in amenities and arts. As jobs and wealth are created, overall well-being increases too.

---

5   Daniel Culbertson, "Indeed's Domestic Migration Survey," Indeed.com, http://blog.indeed.com/2017/05/03/indeed-domestic-migration-survery/.

Our mission, therefore, if we want to increase the vibrancy of our communities, is to help foster these innovation economy jobs. We've discussed why they are good jobs for the workers and great for the companies who hire them, but most importantly, we've seen how an influx of these jobs creates wealth, opportunities, and well-being for others in the community.

But there's one more property of these jobs that's unique to the innovation economy and, as you'll see in this next chapter, a facet that makes them especially crucial in creating opportunities in struggling cities.

SUMMARY

- Companies that lift up local economies sell their products or services nationally or globally, but also create higher wages, more jobs, and wealth for the local community.
- Manufacturing is the best historical example of this, creating a 1.6x job multiplier.
- As low-skilled manufacturing becomes harder to sustain in the United States, innovation economy jobs have taken its place, providing a 5x job multiplier.
- Innovation economy companies require a type of talent that is in short supply: the people it takes to create and rapidly iterate something new, and who in turn attract other people like them.
- Our original research has proven that innovation economy job growth in a city correlates with overall job growth and increased median income—both of which can contribute toward improving quality of life in a community.

CHAPTER 2

IF YOUR CITY ISN'T GROWING, IT'S DYING

*Every moment of one's existence, one is growing
into more or retreating into less. One is always
living a little more or dying a little bit.*

—NORMAN MAILER

It's a crisp March day in Palo Alto, but the air is hot with excitement at the X.com offices. The company, founded by Elon Musk and led by Bill Harris, has just announced major news: they will be merging with their largest competitor, Confinity, to create a powerhouse in the online payment space. Both companies are still small, but each is brimming with talent, and employees believe they could play a major role in the development of online commerce.

History proved them right: this company would soon burst onto the scene under its new name, PayPal, and within three years would sell to eBay for $1.5 billion.[6]

---

6   Margaret Kane, "eBay Picks Up PayPal for $1.5 Billion," Cnet.com, August 18, 2002, https://www.cnet.com/news/ebay-picks-up-paypal-for-1-5-billion/.

Over the next few years, and especially in the months following the company's sale, the original employees left to carve their own paths. With the knowledge, skills, and connections they developed at PayPal, they each had the confidence to create or contribute to new businesses in powerful ways.

Here are a few examples of the impact they've made:

- Elon Musk founded Tesla and SpaceX.
- Steve Chen, Chad Hurley, and Jawed Karim founded You-Tube.
- Reid Hoffman founded LinkedIn.
- Jeremy Stoppelman and Russel Simmons founded Yelp.
- Premal Shah founded Kiva.org.
- David Sacks founded Yammer and Geni.com.
- Peter Thiel started Founders Fund and was the first major investor in Facebook.
- Dave McClure founded 500 Startups and became a legendary angel investor.
- Keith Rabois played major roles at LinkedIn, Slide, Square, and Khosla Ventures.

Out of this small group of brilliant minds with the right support and community, some of the most impactful companies in the world of technology have been born. The group is now commonly referred to as the PayPal Mafia, and members are known among the tech industry for the incredible reach of their impact, as well as their loyalty and support for one another (a theme we will touch on throughout this book).

Not only have these companies' founders impacted the world, but, more importantly for the purposes of this book, they have created an incredible number of innovation economy companies and jobs arising out of their learnings, which originated from being inside a single company.

Each of their new organizations innovated, served a global market, and grew rapidly, creating (in aggregate) hundreds of thousands of innovation economy jobs in the Bay Area. By helping these young minds, and others, to grow into leaders of their own organizations, PayPal created an explosion of opportunities in its local community, which included attracting nonlocal talent to move to the Bay Area to fill these jobs.

PayPal is an extreme example, but this formula holds true on a smaller scale within countless companies and communities. A Twitter thread started by Micah Rosenbloom shared dozens of examples of similar dynamics.[7]

When talented people are given an environment where they can learn, grow, build connections, and generate wealth, they inevitably go on to create new things (and, in turn, produce another environment that fosters more talented people). As this cycle continues, the wealthy winners from previous companies also serve the ecosystem in other ways, investing in new companies, mentoring young leaders, and becoming pillars in the community.

As I flew back and forth across the country, I reflected on the power of this virtuous cycle and the incredible opportunities that the Mohawk Valley and Upstate New York were missing

---

7   This thread is shared with hopes of spurring more research focused on modeling the amount of spin-off company creation rising from exited Innovation Economy Companies. Our More Good Jobs community would participate as a resource to help in such research. https://twitter.com/micahjay1/status/1193981078530342915?s=12.

out on by losing our top tier of young people, leaving to pursue these opportunities elsewhere.

I couldn't help but look at myself, an Upstate New Yorker who had moved to California for fifteen years, becoming responsible for creating what is today more than three thousand jobs across TriNet's offices.

But I was far from being the only person from Upstate who went on to success in creating jobs in the Bay Area or other established tech hubs. Upstate graduates who have created big consumer brands include founders Marc Randolph of Netflix, Andy Rubin of WebTV and Android (before joining Google), Brian Chesky of Airbnb, Jay Walker of Priceline, and Will Glaser of Pandora, to name just a few.

I imagined the impact on our communities if one or more of these founders had created their companies in my home region of Upstate New York rather than in California. Not only in direct job creation, but in the future companies that would be created in the region by the talent that these companies attracted and developed.

Although there are countless roadblocks on the path to becoming a successful entrepreneur, many barriers have been reduced or eliminated in the internet age. Yesterday's industries were asset-intensive and difficult for people early in their career to explore. Today, we've swung to the other end of the spectrum, with inexpensive cloud-based services replacing the need for large upfront investment, easy-to-use tools replacing the need for expensive professionals, and an investor ecosystem with more dollars flowing to founders than ever before. I would argue that today is the greatest time in history to be an entrepreneur.

And yet the largest barrier that holds back potential founders is psychological: if a talented millennial with entrepreneurial aspirations doesn't see successful examples of others who started and grew innovation economy companies in their community, it is natural for them to think they have to move "where the action is"—places like the established startup hubs of Silicon Valley, New York City, Boston, or Austin, to have a chance at success.

WARNING: NOT ALL INDUSTRIES FEED A VIRTUOUS CYCLE

Spinoffs from talent coming out of successful companies is a virtuous cycle that feels almost magical. When I explain the concept to local leaders, they often feel struck by an excitement that changes like these are possible. However, things aren't quite so simple. The cyclical nature of these opportunities isn't a universal truth for all jobs. It's a specific feature of innovation economy companies.

I speak to people all the time who, once hearing about this virtuous cycle, exclaim, "My community has a huge number of jobs in healthcare or government, and a bunch of elite colleges. We should be creating more jobs with these great assets!"

But this isn't the case. The virtuous cycle for growing jobs exists because it's the innovation economy *companies* that have the unique ability to prepare workers for building businesses that create more innovation economy jobs. While becoming a better nurse is an incredibly valuable skill for society, the successful training of nurses doesn't contribute to creating more nursing jobs.

In addition, as we've discussed, the companies creating innovation economy jobs are generating wealth for the community, earning money in what could become a global business, yet having a strong impact on the local economy as they grow. Other jobs—like those in healthcare, government, professional services, and local service businesses—mainly generate their wealth from a local customer base, and therefore aren't bringing new wealth into the local economy.

Because it leads to companies that create more jobs and generate outside wealth, the virtuous cycle we're discussing exists most clearly in the domain of innovation economy companies. This virtuous cycle has all the potential to transform our economy that you might imagine, but this transformation can only come to fruition if we can stimulate the creation of more innovation economy *companies*.

This distinction is particularly true in the world of entrepreneurship. It's clear to most people that there's a substantial difference between a job at an innovative tech startup and a job in local government. But few realize there are differences almost as staggering in the value of jobs in a traditional small business compared with jobs in an early-stage innovation economy company.

By the government's definition, both a coffee shop and an innovative tech startup are classified as small businesses. Yet the needs of the startup (an innovation economy company) are so vastly different from a traditional small business that almost none of the resources provided through the US Small Business Administration, or state and local economic development organizations, are of interest or applicable to startup entrepreneurs.

As a result, our taxpayer resources are directed to traditional small businesses with low job multipliers and miss the huge opportunity to nurture the faster growth of good jobs by supporting innovation economy companies with that 5 to 1 job multiplier.

THE AGGLOMERATION EFFECT

Economists use the term *agglomeration* to describe the situation where forces tend to drive outcomes toward one of two extremes. The economic prospects in our American cities are a case of these agglomeration effects in action.

We spoke in the last chapter about Enrico Moretti, the Berkeley economist who pioneered research on the job multiplier and its impact on cities. His book *The New Geography of Jobs* begins with an exploration of the current state of local economics. Moretti's data backed up my experience: a handful of cities with the right industries and skills were growing good employers and high wages, while cities at the other end of the spectrum, those with shrinking industries and lower presence of in demand workforce skills, were experiencing declining wages and job prospects.

The most important piece of this argument, which we didn't discuss in the last chapter, is that it isn't just a static picture. It's a bifurcation that is accelerating, which is economist speak for saying that instead of a big, static clump in the middle, all activity is pushing cities either in one direction or the other. In short, cities are either moving toward being a Magnet City or on the downhill slide of death as a Talent Exporting City.

One of the most beautiful things about America is the freedom of movement. People (and especially young people) go where they want to go to pursue their greatest opportunities. But as those opportunities increasingly exist within a small number of geographic areas, these successful cities are becoming more successful, while those cities with fewer opportunities are in that downward spiral.

This isn't just true in the innovation economy. Talent flocks to where it sees like-minded people with similar interests and passions. If you want to work in film, you go to LA. Dream of working in finance? Move to New York City. Want to be a country music star? You belong in Nashville.

If you want to start a tech company, there are a handful of cities that most people think are the "right" places to be. These cities attract talent due to the desire to be with like-minded people and great opportunities.

This picture felt all too familiar to me after my years commuting from Upstate New York to Silicon Valley. It seemed that talent was flocking from my hometown area to communities like the Bay Area, where more exciting opportunities existed.

In the years since then, I've learned that this is true statistically as well. As the team I worked with performed the research discussed in the last chapter, we also explored the data around the agglomeration effect. We pondered: *did having more innovation economy jobs predict the number of new innovation economy jobs created?* It turns out that it did.

The cities that had the highest number of innovation economy jobs created more innovation economy jobs each year than those that were starting from a lower total number. This correlation was one of the strongest of any that we researched, with a 0.84 correlation between the two datasets.

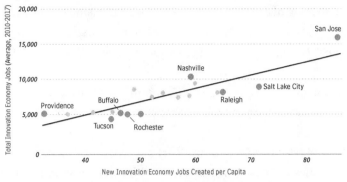

Total Innovation Economy Jobs vs. New Innovation Economy Jobs Created

Source: U.S. Census Bureau, Center for Economic Studies, LEHD

WHAT MAKES A SUCCESSFUL MAGNET CITY?

Our look at the data was convincing about Moretti's finding that US cities are indeed bifurcating into the winners—those with the agglomeration effect working in their favor—and the losers—the rest of the country, shipping their talent off to create wealth and opportunities somewhere else.

We didn't want to understand just the level of agglomeration that was happening. Moretti had already done that beautifully. We wanted to understand *why*. We continued to dig deeper, cross-referencing the Crunchbase dataset with economic trend data, looking for more clues that might point toward forces contributing to the rise of innovation economy companies in a given metro area. What leads to a city ending up on the right side of this divide, growing more innovation economy talent than losing it?

We analyzed the winners and the losers—we chose to label them as Magnet Cities and Talent Exporting Cities—and kept exploring the data for what leading indicators exist for a city to fall into one of these two buckets.

The biggest thing that we kept coming back to was the concentration of recent college graduates heading into innovation economy jobs. If a city was able to *attract talented young people from elsewhere,* the rest of the cycle seemed to flow naturally.

Unfortunately, there isn't a commonly used measure for this attraction of young people, so we decided to create two of them:

1. **Retainment Quotient**: What percentage of the students educated locally who end up working innovation economy jobs stay local for that first job?
2. **Magnet Quotient**: For every hundred thousand students nationwide who end up working innovation economy jobs, how many of them move to the city to take the job?

These two measures—RQ and MQ—became the cornerstone of what we believe can be predictive in determining a city's success with innovation economy companies and jobs.

Your city may show reasonable RQ if you have great amenities and infrastructure coupled with many multiple-generation residents. If your city is losing the top talent needed for next-generation companies, it's akin to filling a leaky bucket not offset by a few incoming arrivals.

Stronger MQ is the trend that will reflect progress in growing innovation economy talent through the agglomeration effect we're describing here.

When a city was high in both of these measures—in the range of 15 percent RQ and 400 MQ or higher—they were sure to show the other attributes, like higher innovation economy jobs and higher median wages, of a Magnet City. When a city failed by these two measurements, the more standard measurements, like job growth and wage trends, were likely to falter as well.

Unsurprisingly, our four cities in the one to two million population bracket with the highest RQ and MQ scores are the exact same as the four cities we looked at earlier that were thriving in regards to innovation economy job growth, overall job growth, and median income: San Jose, Salt Lake City, Nashville, and Raleigh. On the other end of the spectrum, we have the same four cities—Providence, Tucson, Rochester, and Buffalo—that are struggling on these key measures. We will refer back to these two groups of cities throughout the book to illustrate the differences between Magnet Cities and Talent Exporting Cities.

Sometimes it's easier to appreciate our conclusions by looking at the specific data. The first table shows our four strongest Magnet Cities, and it should come as no surprise that their RQ and MQ are also much higher than the nationwide averages of 7 percent and 238 per 100,000, respectively.

TOP MAGNET CITIES WITH ONE TO TWO MILLION POPULATION

	RETAINMENT QUOTIENT (%)	MAGNET QUOTIENT (PER 100,000)
San Jose	20.7	7332
Salt Lake City	23.1	417
Raleigh	13.3	630
Nashville	19.4	400

Contrast this with four of the most Talent Exporting Cities in the population bracket we examined. As you can see, notwithstanding strong local university presence cranking out large numbers of college graduates, these struggling cities have RQs and MQs that tend to be below the average of 7 percent and 238 per 100,000. We decided to include Buffalo as an example, even though its RQ was slightly higher up the list, because it is the largest population center in Upstate New York and has been the recipient of more state-funded economic development than any other city.

TOP TALENT EXPORTING CITIES WITH ONE TO TWO MILLION POPULATION

	RETAINMENT QUOTIENT (%)	MAGNET QUOTIENT (PER 100,000)
Providence	5.4	253
Tucson	4.0	55
Rochester	6.4	114
Buffalo	12.9	78

There are thousands of cities and towns of all sizes all across the country that are struggling with being on the wrong side of the agglomeration effect. They know they are faltering, and they know they want to turn it around, but they aren't sure what to do. It's sad for me to see that, despite our movement in the right direction, Rochester and Buffalo both fall into the camp of cities suffering from these effects.

To turn around all the lagging indicators that we care about—job creation, median wage growth, arts, and culture—we must start by turning around our cities' Retainment Quotient and Magnet Quotient.

This requires facing a difficult truth. All the individuals with high potential who relocated from Talent Exporting Cities to

Magnet Cities made this choice for a reason. I'm one of them. If we want to make our cities hubs that retain our talented young people and attract the best and brightest from elsewhere, we need to learn from today's Magnet Cities and create similar environments where our young people can thrive.

This is a matter of life and death for cities. The bifurcation is growing between thriving cities, generating wealth and well-being for their inhabitants, and the rest of the country, experiencing stagnating wages and growing unemployment and underemployment. If your city is on the wrong side of this divide, things aren't looking good for your city's future residents or leaders.

The purpose of this book is to help draw a roadmap for community leaders interested in and committed to beginning the movement from talent-exporting to Magnet City. That may seem at first like an unachievable task to take on, but as a committed leader, you have the potential to start drawing others into this mission so that, cumulatively, your efforts may contribute toward substantial and potentially multigenerational impact.

And, fortunately, you don't need anyone else's permission to get started.

SUMMARY

- Innovation economy companies engage and develop future leaders to start their own companies, which creates a virtuous cycle.
- The agglomeration effect is in play: cities with lots of innovation economy jobs attract more companies and create more opportunities, while other cities are left behind.
- Our research found that the Retainment Quotient (percentage of college grads in innovation economy jobs who stay in a city) and Magnet Quotient (ratio of college grads nationwide in innovation economy jobs who come to a city) predict how a city will fare in growing more good jobs.
- In the one to two million population range, San Jose, Raleigh, Nashville, and Salt Lake City are Magnet Cities (high RQ and MQ). Providence, Tucson, Buffalo, and Rochester are Talent Exporting Cities (low RQ and MQ).

CHAPTER 3

MAGNET CITIES BREED SUCCESSFUL ENTREPRENEURS. TALENT-EXPORTING COMMUNITIES IMPEDE THEM.

No one saves us but ourselves. No one can and no one may. We ourselves must walk the path.
—GAUTAMA BUDDHA

In the introduction, I shared the story of TriNet's near-failure a year after the business started. Like most first-time entrepreneurs, I started TriNet with an assumption that the accepted practices for a traditional small business would apply to my company. However, the nature of our outsourced HR service was so different from accepted practices of the time that these assumptions weren't serving us.

In retrospect, I can see we were actually an innovation economy startup. Our business model was unheard of in the marketplace because our innovation was aggregating lots of small companies into our group so that TriNet would share in the relationship of being an employer. Our delivery combined HR expertise with back-end technology on an integrated platform to do payroll, benefits, and HR transactions—also unheard of in the small-employer marketplace at the time.

The problem was that we were out in front of the small business market that wasn't yet ready to buy into our innovation. Even though we were pedaling hard to expand our base of local small business relationships, we were dead stuck in not being able to get traction because reluctant small business owners were all looking to see evidence of TriNet's model being adopted by someone else first.

Just like today's innovation economy startups that can't find customer traction, after a year of frustrating and anemic sales effort, our approach was a resounding failure and we were running out of cash.

Given our dearth of sales and marketing resources, we decided that a different path to building a base of raving fan customers would be to pivot away from selling to the general small business community and instead target the narrow vertical market in which our services would have the strongest appeal.

TriNet's narrowing focus allowed us to scale faster by rapidly customizing our service offering to meet the unique needs of our chosen market and, importantly, generate referrals from happy customer entrepreneurs who would be in contact with other similarly situated entrepreneurs in that target market.

This approach seems obvious in retrospect, but at the time, it was unheard of. Building scale quickly is critical for professional employer organizations (PEOs) like TriNet, since doing so is the only path to delivering the stated value proposition of large group purchasing power and spreading systems investment and expertise across an ever-expanding group of small companies.

The greatest benefit of all was one that I couldn't have predicted. Unlike the business environments I'd experienced in the past, targeting the startup community environment was the perfect place for an emerging innovation-based business like ours to find prospective customers.

Even though this was pre-internet, the events for startup entrepreneurs and the people and companies who supported them were open and publicly visible so I could always find them. Many of these events were filled with great people. And, most importantly, people were willing to talk, share, and help each other out *before trust was earned*.

At the traditional chamber of commerce meetups I'd previously attended, business owners would turn away when I explained my new idea. It seemed that too few people had time or interest to learn more about something they had never heard of before.

In the startup community, the fact that nobody had heard about PEOs didn't deter them from wanting to know more. They were curious and open enough to new ideas that they would almost always ask questions, so it became a true dialogue instead of a pitch.

Sometimes, after as little as five to ten minutes of conversation, the person I had just met would introduce me to someone else in the room who might be a potential customer or some other resource who could help me.

There was this atmosphere in the community where the ethos was to help people who were starting and growing innovation companies. If you could help someone, you were expected to, and there wasn't an expectation that they needed to return the favor. Everyone understood that when we're all helping each other, more good things happen.

This attitude wasn't limited to tech company entrepreneurs. I saw lawyers, consultants, accountants, and other service providers adopt the same mindset, as they were also selling to the same community *and that is how the startup community works.*

It was contagious, and soon I was in the fold, making connections and helping entrepreneurs and other community supporters I had just met, while having no clear expectation of them giving back to me.

These relationships were what kept TriNet growing as we made the transition to focus on emerging tech customers. Strangers introduced me to other strangers in a pay-it-forward fashion, and those connections became the backbone of our approach to customer acquisition, problem solving, and even fundraising.

Compare this to the prevailing attitudes in Talent Exporting Communities. Even today, in my home area of Upstate New York, we struggle to create an environment in which entrepreneurs and service providers support each other in the way I was supported in my early days in Silicon Valley decades ago.

Local communities are quick to blame government or lack of investment capital, but as you'll see in the chapters to follow, the core of what makes job-generating communities different is much simpler: it's the attitude and mindset of all those who can give.

But before we can get there, we must first dive into at least a short peek into some other big-picture forces impeding high-growth entrepreneurship in the innovation economy from taking root in Talent Exporting Communities and states.

Reader alert: The next few sections of this chapter are not pleasant. Try as I might to keep things on a constructive path, what follows here is necessary context that sets the stage for the rest of the book being solutions-oriented. So stay with me through this chapter and, once we get to chapter 4, we'll be on an upbeat path as we look at alternatives and solutions to address the challenging circumstances faced by those in Talent Exporting Communities.

HOW GOVERNMENT IMPEDES GROWTH OF INNOVATION ECONOMY ENTREPRENEURS

Most of the elected officials I've met are well-intentioned and truly want to do what they can to help stimulate job growth. The traditional paths for government to do so are through a combination of how they allocate our tax dollars for economic development and also the laws and regulations they approve with the intent of stimulating job growth.

There are two core problems we see on both of these paths. The first is the common belief it is possible to create new jobs from the top down. Politicians tend to see job growth as something predictable and under their control, so we often encounter what I'll refer to as the *Field of Dreams* mentality. Think, "If we build [insert factory, office building, etc.], the jobs will follow." At an abstract level, this sounds completely logical—except that it doesn't work in reality.

Couple the "build it and they will come" belief with the short-term focus politicians have in order to impress voters before the next election cycle, and you have a recipe for a lot of impressive-seeming actions without substantial results.

One way this combination of beliefs manifests itself is in how politicians covet building physical infrastructure, thinking this is the path to lure companies into a community to create jobs.

They do this because that's what they've done for the last fifty years, and it fits the mold of top-down behaviors that look good in a press release. In using this approach for new innovation economy companies, they're trying to solve today's problem with an old set of tools.

While I am all for the idea of making smart infrastructure investments, I would argue that putting politicians in charge of deciding which companies will be the beneficiaries of public support is a slippery slope, with economic consequences that are rarely transparent. Consequently, taxpayers don't fully grasp the magnitude of tax dollars invested per job created or have awareness of any other alternatives that might grow more jobs. Instead, all attention is given to the ribbon-cutting photo op with a collection of politicians vying for the opportunity to lay claim in saying, "Look at what I did for you."

Our governor in New York puts all his emphasis on publicizing the billions of dollars spent from the budget on economic development, as if our state spending is the most important metric to be flaunted in showing progress.

The only time we hear about output measures like actual jobs created from these billions comes when a big project fails or an enterprising reporter starts digging to compare actual jobs created with the original projections in the press releases that announced a big government-funded project.

CENTRAL NEW YORK FILM HUB: FALLACY OF "BUILD IT AND THEY WILL COME"

In 2014, Governor Andrew Cuomo announced with great fanfare the creation of the Central New York Film Hub, based in Syracuse. He projected that the $15 million in taxpayer funds being invested to construct a new facility would create more than 350 high-tech jobs by having a university-operated hub blend cutting-edge nanotechnology with film production.

Three years after opening, the gleaming fifty-two thousand square foot building sat virtually empty, having been used for a few short projects, never coming close to living up to the governor's hype of "Hollywood comes to Onondaga" (County).

In 2018, after failing to secure commercial tenants or traction with film projects, the state transferred title to the facility to Onondaga County for one dollar, effectively writing off the $15 million taxpayer investment in the ill-conceived belief that the government can create businesses and jobs by funding construction of a building.

New York State has many such examples of failed publicly funded construction efforts in the name of job creation, but this one stands out not just for being an illustrative bust, but for the sordid view into how cozy relationships between politicians and property developers also have potential for corruption to creep in.

In this case, COR Development Company was the governor's largest campaign contributor at the time and also the sole firm to submit a bid on the $15 million project. Investigations by US and local prosecutors eventually revealed a bid-rigging scheme involving the developer and several individuals having close relationships with the governor. Thus far, three convictions with prison terms have been handed down.

Another all too common approach is to play the game of business attraction, cutting a special deal with a large company to open up a new facility (in particular one with manufacturing) in a Talent Exporting City desperate for job growth. Business attraction usually involves some combination of publicly funded building construction, infrastructure for the area where the facility is located, and tax incentives beneficial to the business moving in.

These deals are announced by politicians, with lots of hoopla celebrating the success of job creation that hasn't happened yet. If the commercial venture actually proceeds, there are new rounds of publicity with the ribbon-cutting photo ops at groundbreaking, then facility opening. In each wave of press, politicians battle to get credit for how they were responsible for creating jobs.

What gets lost is the comparison over time between the original job projections and what ultimately happens if the project is completed (which doesn't always happen) or when the tax incentives expire.

Patterns of "build it and they will come" and "business attraction" are not unique to New York State. They are repeated all over the country. Politicians allocate taxpayer dollars to build a building in a heartbeat, but that effort does nothing to actually create jobs beyond the construction phase nor does it have any impact on accelerating the launch of new startup companies.

A recent paper from researchers at Columbia Business School and Princeton investigated this problem.[8] The researchers found no evidence that tax incentives given to individual companies increased overall economic growth. Furthermore, the study found that almost a third of total state incentive spending "went to .0072% of new firms and 1.41% of all jobs created by those firms."

The economic environment of Talent Exporting Cities typically features low-cost real estate already, so with startups having nominal space requirements to begin with, cheap rent, even in a new facility, is almost a nonfactor in where the entrepreneur will site the business.

So is advertising touting low cost, quality of life, or fill-in-the-blank local attributes that won't move the needle when the best local talent needed for innovation is not sticking around.

PUBLIC MONEY GOING INTO PRIVATE COMPANIES

There is a long history of government funding research targeting healthcare, environment, defense, or other societal needs that might be aided by the research. While it makes sense to allocate some public dollars toward research being conducted

---

8   Cailin R. Slattery and Owen M. Zidar, "Evaluating State and Local Business Tax Incentives," NBER Working Paper No. 26603, January 2020, https://www.nber.org/papers/w26603.

by colleges and companies, a grayer area creeps in when public funds go into commercializing a new technology by a private company.

The attractiveness from a political standpoint is clear: let the government write a check to a company as part of an economic development effort to create jobs.

The problem is that this then puts the government in a position to be picking the winners, a task that raises the same set of problems as the "build it and they will come" and "business attraction" ploys. History has shown us that the government's track record for picking winners is horrible. Professional investors with their own money at stake have a hard enough time predicting which companies will grow. Even the best professional startup investors in the world pick more losers than winners. To expect a government bureaucrat to be able to outperform these investors is ridiculous.

As millions in state penalties loom, Tesla says it's hiring hundreds in Buffalo

—ALBANY BUSINESS REVIEW, JANUARY 30, 2020

Tesla has said it is hiring "hundreds" at its state-owned solar panel factory in Buffalo months ahead of its deadline to create 1,460 jobs or face millions in state penalties.

Elon Musk said in a conference call with investors on Wednesday that the Tesla factory in Buffalo—what the company calls Gigafactory 2—is "doing great" with little detail of what that actually means.

The factory in Buffalo's south end was the centerpiece of Gov. Andrew Cuomo's Buffalo Billion plan. The state spent $750 million to build the factory on brownfield land remediated from a former steel mill. In exchange, SolarCity (which was eventually acquired by Tesla) promised 5,000 high-paying, high-tech jobs upstate—3,000 of them in Buffalo.

Tesla is still ramping up Buffalo production of its solar roof tiles, a product Musk said would be revolutionary. And it has been short of its 2020 job creation goals there.

The factory was also at the center of a corruption case and eventual felony convictions of SUNY Poly CEO Alain Kaloyeros and three developers for rigging bids on the Buffalo project and others across upstate.

Employment at the Buffalo factory must reach 1,460—almost double what it was last summer—by April, or Tesla will have to pay a $41.2 million penalty to the state for each year it falls short. Tesla and its partner, Panasonic, had about 800 employees at the site last summer. Musk did not provide an update on how many employees are at the site now during the investor call on Wednesday.

A Vanity Fair story in August found the state quietly changed the requirements Tesla must meet in exchange for its $1 lease on the Buffalo factory. The requirement for 1,460 "high-tech" jobs at the factory was watered down to jobs of any type. An agreement to hire 900 people at the factory within two years of construction ending in 2017 changed to 500. And the timing for creating additional jobs was extended to 10 years after the factory was completed.

A DOCILE POPULACE WAITS FOR GOVERNMENT TO LEAD

After many decades of strong government intervention such as we see in Upstate New York, I've come to observe a lulling of general public awareness about nongovernment pathways to actually play a role in contributing toward job growth.

Some of that is due to local media fixation on anything that is messaged by government officials while ignoring trends going on in the business world, such as actual developments involving innovation economy companies right in their community.

The prevailing attitude inside our Talent Exporting Communities seems to be "There's nothing I can do—it's in the hands of our government to fix this mess." Sadly, I hear this refrain even from high-level business executives and other entrepreneurs: the very people who are in a position to help lead change are instead resigning themselves to the belief that our dire circumstances are someone else's responsibility to fix.

Despite all this, politicians need not be the enemy when it comes to creating good jobs. When they take the long-term view and understand the needs of entrepreneurs, public officials can be strong allies. Most of them got into politics because they truly care about helping people, and if you help them see a better path to serve the community, some will get on board in ways that may support your job-growth ambition. We'll cover specific paths to engage government in chapter 10.

ENTREPRENEURSHIP IS HARDER IN TALENT EXPORTING CITIES

We know that creating more innovation economy jobs in Talent Exporting Cities requires getting more startups launched. But starting businesses in these communities is challenging. Businesses in less entrepreneurial areas lack something essential, something businesses in entrepreneurially dense areas rely upon: an open and connected community of entrepreneurs to lean on for support.

It is true that we live in a connected age. Many businesses are now born from a laptop and an idea, and location is less of a factor in successfully starting up than it has been in the past.

Yet new Innovation Economy Companies have an incredibly high failure rate, and those who succeed can almost always point to others in their community who helped them succeed through mentorship, capital, customers, referral sources, or partner companies. Starting a business is a networked activity. Your low odds of success become even lower if you don't have a community to plug into the things you need to grow the company.

Our mainstream narrative is that businesses survive and grow on the brilliance and hard work of their founders. This is a limited view shaped by our media and entertainment. In most cases, businesses succeed and fail based on their leader's ability to connect with the specific people they need to support them. This is especially true for first-time founders, who don't have access to many of the resources needed to build a company. The open and connected community of entrepreneurs in Silicon Valley led to the clients that allowed TriNet to take off and get through the challenges in our early days. But I was also aided by mentors, assisted in raising capital, and connected with valuable partners because this network existed. Without the benefits of this community, TriNet wouldn't have succeeded.

No matter how whiz-bang the innovation, a company can't get off the ground without customers, mentors, and capital. Once it's launched, it cannot reach the next level without an incredible team. The network surrounding the entrepreneur is the accelerant for finding each of these valuable connections that are critical to the company's success.

If we're going to spur entrepreneurship in the areas that need it most, we need to accept how significant these connections are. You can't just throw up a website and go. Real, personal connections are the fuel that supports startup launch and growth.

HOW VISIBLE ARE THE ENTREPRENEURS?

These connections are more difficult to come by in a Talent Exporting City. Whereas I was able to lead TriNet to make those connections in Silicon Valley—which eventually led to us hiring thousands of employees and generating millions of dollars in revenue for the local economy—a hypothetical TriNet startup in Upstate New York launched with what I knew back then never would have gotten off the ground.

Even with the same vision or perseverance I had at the time, if I had been in Upstate New York I never would have had the critical access to the people I needed to meet, who would in turn lead me to customers, investors, mentors, and team members essential for me to grow an innovation economy startup.

As we discussed in the previous chapters, the success and growth of innovative companies are the fuel that creates good jobs, bringing money into the local community to create more jobs and develop young professionals with the skills and wealth to either become entrepreneurs or support entrepreneurship, which continues the cycle.

The most critical connection resource of all would be finding the community of seasoned entrepreneurs, startups, and other qualified supporters to plug into.

Sounds easy, but here are a few quick reminders of the structural impediments:

- A Talent Exporting City's population is likely lulled into waiting for government to solve the problem.
- There is a dearth of peer innovation economy startups to connect with, much less successful leaders who can share relevant high-growth experience.
- Those entrepreneurs who have reached success in traditional industries may feel that they don't have much to contribute toward helping an innovation economy startup, or that they don't have enough pathways bringing them into personal contact with startup founders to appreciate those with highest potential for success.
- Since the government and media don't talk about these forces, local skepticism can be widespread from those who don't yet understand how innovation economy opportunities could work in the community.
- The most successful local entrepreneurs can be so besieged with requests that some send "do not disturb" signals or, even worse, relocate out of the area following the sale of their company. (New York State seems to take particular pride in pushing out our wealthiest citizens, who then become investors in other states.)

All of these become roadblocks or impediments to today's startup entrepreneur "finding their tribe," so necessary to start the long and risky journey of building an innovation economy company.

The question becomes: where are the entrepreneurs in Talent Exporting Cities and how can we get them engaged?

The fortunate answer is that in work throughout all eight metro areas Upstate Venture Connect has supported, we've been able to identify entrepreneurs who can be mobilized, but it required a concentrated effort to find and nurture their awareness of the opportunity to collaborate in ways that are mutually beneficial.

Yet because these places lack a connected entrepreneurial community, new entrepreneurs have a much harder time finding seasoned mentors and people who can and want to help them, compared to what would happen if they happened to be in a Magnet City like Silicon Valley, New York metro, or Boston.

Without easy opportunities to meet a network of potential role models, mentors, and capital providers, the would-be entrepreneurs in Talent Exporting Cities feel kneecapped in their attempts to launch and grow, so they take the plunge and move to a Magnet City.

Young entrepreneurs face a difficult challenge when confronting that kind of attitude: stay local and accept even lower odds of success, or vote with their feet and move to an area where a supportive community is both *visible* and *accessible*.

Many make the second choice, and as that cycle plays out, it worsens the community they left behind, making it harder for future entrepreneurs in their hometown to launch a true startup.

The loss of each aspiring innovation economy entrepreneur further reduces the potential to start growing more innovation economy jobs, needed to slow the decline of the community's talent exporting cycle.

MINORITY ENTREPRENEURS ARE ESPECIALLY DISADVANTAGED IN TALENT EXPORTING CITIES

An insufficient pool of experienced entrepreneurs to help mentor and connect the next-generation startup creates an even bigger obstacle for those who are disadvantaged by being people of color. Not only are all the forces we've described to this point at work, but minority entrepreneurs are too often outside the network where the most successful people in the community come together to interact and help each other.

Talent-exporting cities can have proud pasts that may include clinging to traditions from an earlier industrial era. A community's power network may still be gathering at private clubs, golf courses, or other member-only groups that, while not explicitly excluding minorities, may have little to no participation from the minority community. Unlike forums in Magnet Cities, there may be a lack of open, community-wide gatherings to present opportunities for top leaders and aspiring entrepreneurs to interact in person with enterprising entrepreneurs outside their existing social groups.

If you're that promising minority entrepreneur looking to find people to help you grow your startup, the path to get referred in to the network of highly influential people (HIPs) can feel out of reach. Not only might you lack access points, but since the community hasn't experienced startup success yet, there may be no other minority-led startups or companies from which you can get the needed guidance on navigating the local power network.

A *Harvard Business Review* article,[9] "The Other Diversity Dividend," helps put into perspective the unplanned but very real effect of a network's lack of diversity creating barriers that impede a minority entrepreneur's ability to get funded by venture capital. Authors Paul Gompers and Silpa Kovvali note:

> The gender and racial makeup of the venture capital industry is staggeringly homogeneous. A comprehensive dataset of every VC organization and investor in the United States since 1990 shows that the industry has remained relatively uniform for the past 28 years. Only 8% of the investors are women. Racial minorities are also underrepresented—about 2% of VC investors are Hispanic, and fewer than 1% are black. Those groups have seen significantly increased representation in other fields and in advanced professional and scientific degree programs, but not in the VC industry. It's against that backdrop that venture capitalists choose their collaborators at other firms, investing their money side by side and joining the boards that guide the start-ups. Most investors specialize in a particular industry or sector, so potential partners are easy for researchers like us to identify: They are investing in the same types of deals at around the same time. And venture capitalists are far more likely to partner with people if they share their gender or race. They're also significantly more likely to collaborate with people if they share their educational background or a previous employer. Belonging to the same racial group increases the propensity to work together by 39.2%, and having a degree from the same school increases it by 34.4%. Not only is the likelihood of collaborating on any one deal greater, but VCs tend to keep teaming up with those who share their traits.

---

9   Paul Gompers and Silpa Kovvali, "The Other Diversity Dividend," *Harvard Business Review*, July 2018, https://hbr.org/2018/07/the-other-diversity-dividend.

IT'S TIME TO BREAK THE CYCLE

Over the past few chapters, we've built a connection among a few concepts that you may not have seen as related before reading this book.

To recap: we all want more good jobs, and we know that top-down attempts to create good jobs don't tend to be effective. Rather, job growth comes from wealth flowing into the local economy in industries that have a high "multiplier"—a measurement that represents the number of new jobs generated for each worker in a specific field. Historically, manufacturing supported communities with a multiplier of 1.6x. Today, we have an even greater opportunity, as what we're calling innovation economy jobs have a staggering multiplier of 5x.

Given all this, efforts to generate good jobs as a whole should focus on increasing the number of innovation economy companies, and resulting innovation economy jobs are generated by facilitating more entrepreneurs in scalable businesses, who then support those starting up, to increase everyone's odds of success.

We also discussed the virtuous cycle: entrepreneurship tends to breed more entrepreneurship, and startup teams develop employees in a context to gain financial stability, understanding, and experience to be prepared to start and grow their own businesses. Successful businesses within a community beget more successful businesses, so any work we do to increase the success of local entrepreneurs will give us more than our money's worth of results.

Lastly, we've examined the idea that entrepreneurs don't succeed in a bubble. Despite the myth of the solo entrepreneur succeeding without any support, the reality is that all innovative businesses need the right connections to survive—it's the personal connections leading to customers, capital, talent, and mentorship that make all the difference in navigating from a company concept to actual traction in the marketplace.

So, finally, we've arrived at a clear directive for those of us who want to create more good jobs: if we want to create good jobs, we need to build communities that connect new entrepreneurs to the resources that they need in order to succeed and grow.

The rest of this book is your roadmap for how to do that in your community.

This is within our grasp. It's just a matter of building a community that entices the future entrepreneurs, the job creators of tomorrow, to stay.

There's nothing in the soil of Silicon Valley that makes it a better home for our young people. They've simply built the culture, from the ground up, that allows bright people to thrive, and eventually, some of them become outsized job creators even with companies you've never heard of.

We can do the same.

SUMMARY

- One of the greatest factors in whether an entrepreneur will succeed is whether they have a supportive entrepreneurial community around them.
- This makes entrepreneurship more challenging in Talent Exporting Cities, where there are few role models and it is hard for founders to find help or talent for their most pressing priorities.
- This is made worse because Talent Exporting Cities don't tend to have a culture where successful entrepreneurs make themselves available to help new entrepreneurs.
- Closed networks of community leaders inside a Talent Exporting City further impede the opportunity to benefit from the potential that minority entrepreneurs present for the community.
- To turn our Talent Exporting Cities into Magnet Cities, we need to facilitate changing the local environment to embrace the opportunities leaders have to help startup founders.

PART 2

CREATING A MAGNET CITY CULTURE

CHAPTER 4

CREATING A COMMUNITY THAT FOSTERS RELATIONSHIPS

Some of the biggest challenges in relationships come from the fact that most people enter a relationship in order to get something: they're trying to find someone who's going to make them feel good. In reality, the only way a relationship will last is if you see your relationship as a place that you go to give, and not a place that you go to take.

—TONY ROBBINS

Despite all the modern advances, including the miracle that is the internet, I would posit that our most impactful relationships can still be traced back to connections that have origins in a real-time conversation—especially from face-to-face conversation.

For a new entrepreneur breaking into the scene without many connections, the question arises: how do they go about meeting people they don't yet know or have a connection to?

Based on dozens of experiments run over ten years in building the Upstate Venture Connect startup ecosystem to more than seventeen thousand people, our conclusion is that the most productive path to foster high-impact connections is total focus on *scaling up volume and quality* on just two avenues: creative collisions and referrals by trusted source.

CREATIVE COLLISIONS

By creative collisions, I refer to the "by chance" meetings that occur when you happen to be in a room with someone who has the potential to help you. Collisions take place at industry events, happy hours, speeches, or any other location where like-minded people congregate. They are right-place-at-the-right-time kind of meetings, and as you collide unexpectedly with others, most people will be willing to talk in those circumstances, as you have something in common as a reason for being there.

Say you're at a cocktail hour, standing at your table enjoying your snack and adult beverage, when you notice the person standing next to you is from XYZ venture capital firm. You strike up a conversation and, after a few minutes, are deep in conversation about your business.

That's a creative collision. If you sent an email or called that same person on the phone and asked for a meeting, they would say no (or, more likely, their gatekeeper assistant would screen you out before you even connected with them). But, because you're standing next to them in an open environment, it's a completely different dynamic. You have the opportunity to advance a dialogue that otherwise wouldn't have taken place.

REFERRAL BY TRUSTED SOURCE

When I say referral by trusted source, I'm referring to introductions made by someone whose opinions are highly valued enough that the two people being connected are likely to engage based on their mutual connection with the referring party.

Let's continue the example from the cocktail hour. As you speak with your new friend from XYZ venture capital firm, you tell him the struggles you're facing getting your sales process in order. He smiles and says, "I've got the answer for you," before turning around and yelling, "Hey, Teresa, do you have a minute for me to introduce someone?"

When Teresa arrives, your friend explains that she's the founder of a quickly growing company that just went through similar struggles in their sales process. He gives her an overview of your business and what you're struggling with, and then leaves you and Teresa to connect and discuss. Because of his excitement and recommendation, Teresa is thrilled to help you out.

That's a referral by trusted source. Even though you'd only met a few minutes earlier, you trusted your new friend enough to be interested in meeting Teresa. As importantly, Teresa trusted him enough to be willing to help you out.

Another variation of referral by trusted source can come through two parties being part of an organization that holds a high standard for entry and members feel affinity toward each other even if they've never met. If you're a Harvard alum and another Harvard alum you don't know reaches out to you with a question, there's a good chance you'll actually think about responding.

Curated networks take all kinds of forms beyond college alumni, and as we've found in Upstate Venture Connect, it is possible to create one from scratch. We do so by following the principles of exclusivity, affinity, and pathways for those in the network to find each other so they in turn can make a referral by trusted source without ever having met the person being contacted.

THE SPARK THAT LIT TRINET

In her excellent book *Regional Advantage: Culture and Competition in Silicon Valley and Route 128,* the economist AnnaLee Saxenian examines how the center of gravity of the computing industry shifted from Boston to Silicon Valley over the course of just two decades.

She concluded that a major reason Silicon Valley thrived was the culture, particularly a culture of trust. In Boston, you had to earn trust before anyone would help you. If you were new or unknown, people were reluctant to risk their reputation by introducing you to their peers until you had proven yourself. In Silicon Valley, by contrast, there was deep receptivity to new ideas and willingness to open personal networks to support others *before trust was earned.*

My experience as a rookie entrepreneur in Silicon Valley absolutely validated Saxenian's finding of this important cultural distinction.

Before I started TriNet, I attended many industry conferences and saw how companies discouraged their employees from being open with people working at other companies who might have been potential competitors. It was common to bump into people who would happily ask questions to get info but seemed to offer little in return about either their challenges or solutions, much less how they might help me.

By contrast, the Silicon Valley community was open and connected. Engineers from competing companies would have drinks together and talk about problems they were trying to solve, entrepreneurs would provide introductions freely, and everyone was open to new ideas.

This was essential to TriNet's early success. As we worked to sign our initial customers, it was difficult to get people on board with the new idea of outsourced HR. What we were doing deviated from industry norms, and we were working in an industry that required a lot of trust because we represented the customer in handling money and elements of their employee relationships on the company's behalf. You can't get any more sacred than that. When we tried to sell the same service to the general small business community, we ran into a wall. Business owners would simply tell me they couldn't take the risk, and to come back when the model was proven. With the stakes so high for them, this wasn't an entirely irrational position to take.

Only when we started working in the true Silicon Valley community—the community of emerging technology companies—were we able to overcome this hurdle. First, the sheer number of people I was able to meet grew substantially. Silicon Valley had a constant stream of events, groups, and organizations that allowed me to meet founders by having creative collisions with them. I entered the market with very few connections but, just by virtue of being in the same rooms with people again and again, was able to start growing a high-impact personal network over a relatively short time period.

One organization that was particularly fruitful was the Silicon Valley Association of Startup Entrepreneurs (SVASE). They welcomed all comers with a philosophy of inclusion. It was through a creative collision at an SVASE event that I met Bob Ulrich, a partner at Vanguard Venture Partners. Through our conversation, he developed an interest in TriNet, as Vanguard had some HR and benefit needs that I represented we might help address.

A few weeks later I was in the hot seat in front of all four Vanguard general partners, explaining why moving their payroll to TriNet was the right choice and easing their fears around the risks.

Over the course of that conversation, I recognized that the people I was meeting with had a different attitude than the general small business community. Rather than telling me that what I proposed was too risky, they were receptive enough to the idea to look hard at it. They got curious, asked questions, and evaluated the risk for themselves. We ended up signing the account, and this cycle began repeating with other interactions from both creative collisions and slowly building toward referral by trusted source.

With more personal interactions, more people were willing to introduce me to peers who might benefit from TriNet. Nobody was scared that if they introduced a friend to me at an event, they would be blamed for the riskiness of TriNet's business. We all understood that most of the businesses in the room were innovative and had some element of risk—after all, that's exactly the basis for creating innovation in the first place!

Referrals continued to escalate once I had a few Silicon Valley reference accounts. After we worked with the team at Vanguard and impressed them with our service, they began to refer their portfolio companies. Those companies would refer us to their friends and colleagues. I saw that my primary focus should be to go out, identify, and educate other trusted sources to do the same that Vanguard did.

As this continued, the risk perceived by the initial doubters dissipated, and within a few short years hundreds of Silicon Valley companies were using the TriNet platform.

Without those referrals by trusted sources, many potential customers would have brushed us off the same way that the general small business community had done in our very early days. But because of the Silicon Valley culture of give first introductions and referrals, we were able to get in the door with the people we needed to reach.

The same principles hold with many other types of relationships that I needed to succeed. Through the same two channels—creative collisions and referrals by trusted sources—I was able to meet the people I needed to connect with to raise money, to get professional services, to hire talent, and to find great mentors.

HOW CAN WE INCREASE CREATIVE COLLISIONS?

Founders, especially young founders, are often hungry for the types of events that support creative collisions. They intuitively know that their business prospects will be improved by the serendipitous connections they can make, so they're always looking for new ways to meet interesting people.

Unfortunately, in many cities, it isn't so easy. To make these powerful connections, the places where the community is hanging out need to be visible and accessible to newcomers. If the aspiring entrepreneur doesn't know where to plug in, the potential for creative collisions is lost.

Creative collisions are a volume game. We need to have many creative collisions to see the value they provide. It's almost impossible for the young entrepreneur to intentionally go out and find the few people he or she needs to meet. Instead, young entrepreneurs succeed at networking by taking a lot of shots on goal, knowing that some pucks (although they don't know which) will end up in the net.

For these reasons, the most important thing we can do to increase creative collisions is to create *consistent, open,* in-person events and publicize them broadly.

Why do these events need to be consistent? Although one-time events do a great job of generating PR and getting many people out of the house, they don't have as much of an impact on creative collisions as do recurring events that bring a good number of the same group together.

When the same group appears again and again at these consistent events, newcomers are able to establish credibility by showing up multiple times. At any one-time event, you might get lucky and run into someone, but if you are able to show up multiple times, you're able to make the transition from outsider to insider. Consistency allows that to happen.

Why do events need to be open? One of the problems I often see when organizations or individuals take responsibility for creating more consistent events in their community is that they try to keep things exclusive. Organizations have a vested interest to serve their constituents, and the paid staff who may be leading and marketing the event too often want to limit attendees to the organization's defined constituents.

I see this frequently with local colleges who say they are keen to spur entrepreneurship in their communities. When they do put on an event, they'll often market to, if not limit attendees to, students, alumni, and faculty. These divisions close off the community and make such events less valuable than they could be if they were marketed to and welcomed all interested comers beyond the boundaries of the college.

The events that generate the most successful creative collisions are open to the public, and information about the events is distributed broadly to the community at large.

There are hundreds of possible formats for consistent, open, in-person activities. Many of the most successful focus specifically on sharing knowledge from experienced, successful entrepreneurs that is valuable to aspiring and early-stage entrepreneurs. This format attracts the founders hungriest to learn and gives them a great way to get more out of the event than just the potential for creative collisions.

The tech meetup format is one of the most popular ways to do this. It comes in many flavors, but the idea is that you'll have some combination of community announcements, education through speeches, panels, or pitches, as well as some designated social time. This allows you to nail down a concrete format and do the event on a regularly scheduled basis (say, once a month) so that the community knows what to expect and when.

The interactions between entrepreneurs and investors are particularly important at these events. Investors are frequently sources of advice, connections, and capital—three of the largest constraints facing early-stage startups. Some events facilitate these introductions by organizing pitches from local startups, with more seasoned entrepreneurs and investors attending to hear the pitches and look for investment opportunities. With an added social opportunity to make connections, this is a valuable format for bringing two spheres of the community together.

An additional avenue Upstate Venture Connect (UVC) took to broaden awareness of startup community events was to publish an online events calendar for the entire Upstate region. Users choose to sort the calendar by location and tags for zooming in to their specific interests. Organizations looking to spread the word of their events have an easy path to post on this calendar. Since many of these organizations don't have an easily maintainable calendar on their own website, UVC provides a downloadable widget allowing the organization to embed the events calendar on the organization's own website. This can include a customizable sort, putting their community or organization as the default view while still allowing regional events to be accessed by their site visitors. The net effect of this approach is that the UVC events calendar has grown to be the most highly trafficked section of our site—in turn providing engagement of both new and returning site visitors (visit UVC.org/events).

COLLISIONS THROUGH VIRTUAL MEETINGS

Prior to the 2020 pandemic, I would not have mentioned virtual meetings as a plausible place to spark creative collisions. One-to-one in-person contact is the very foundation of my thesis for the value of getting the right people into the same room.

The pandemic drove a change in behaviors because everyone was hunkered down at home and precluded from attending public events of any kind. Starting in March 2020, meetings—both personal and group—suddenly all shifted to online, now including large numbers of people who had little experience in virtual meetings suddenly forced to adapt to a new virtual world.

We know that post-pandemic restoration of public and in-person meetings will come back, but there will also be a heightened level of public acceptance of virtual meetings that we didn't have before. We'll also see a number of new technologies around improved user interface and user experience focused on making virtual meetings more productive than ever before—improvements hatched by the next wave of innovation economy entrepreneurs needing support from their communities.

So while we're still early in that evolution when this book goes to print, my observation is changing about the potential for collisions to be sparked in virtual group meetings. I'm noticing that virtual group meetings that are done by video and are part of a recurring group gathering as described above are helping me lay sufficient foundation to strike up a dialogue with people I've not yet met in person. The most effective approaches to make that happen go beyond speaker presentations to include thoughtful facilitation that directs and controls group interaction, moving in and out of breakout rooms and orchestrating one-on-one private sessions of attendees. All of this will continue to evolve as I expect virtual gatherings to become an increasingly common asset in the toolbox of organizers building startup community.

There is no magic in building more creative collisions in your community. With recurring, open, in-person events that stay true to innovation economy themes, people find each other, and that's where the magic happens.

HOW CAN WE INCREASE REFERRALS FROM TRUSTED SOURCES?

With all the creative collisions happening at these events, early-stage entrepreneurs will benefit tremendously from the new connections they're building (which increases the success of companies and thus the number of good jobs). However, as we discussed, creative collisions are like shots on goal—it's a volume game, as most won't work out. The real exponential benefit comes when those new collisions start the process of beginning a relationship that evolves into a trusted source who provides referrals.

This is one of the attributes that made Silicon Valley so successful. In great communities like Silicon Valley, referrals are made quickly. Individuals don't feel they are putting their reputation on the line by making a referral. They don't feel that you have to earn it. Instead, when they think that a connection may lead to an interesting result, they are quick to make it. These low-barrier connections were what allowed me to quickly meet my early TriNet clients, and they've benefited thousands of other companies based in Silicon Valley too.

Increasing the number of referrals by trusted sources in your community isn't as easy as putting on more events. It's a subtler, more human thing to impact. But it's possible.

There are two things we can do to increase the number of high-quality referrals. Although not fast or easy, the best thing we can do is to play the long game in working toward building a culture, like Silicon Valley's, that expects and rewards people for providing introductions. More readily, we can build referral networks to explicitly encourage this behavior.

CULTURE

Let's talk first about culture. Changing the culture in any community is a long-term effort. Culture can't just be dictated and adopted en masse. Instead, it must emerge organically, as a result of the way people in the community are treated. This leads to an important conclusion: to create a specific culture, the best things you can do are to *live the culture* and *reward the culture*.

Leaders in the communities that have succeeded in creating a high referral density always seem to echo a consistent mantra: give first.[10] By giving constantly, without expectation of return, they imbue the rest of the community with a similar mindset. Through their actions, they impact people's perception of what a successful business leader is, one relationship at a time. They show younger leaders that the referrals they're providing aren't transactional, aimed at self-promotion. Instead, they are

---

10   Tamara Chuang, "How Techstars' GiveFirst Mantra Became a Road Map for the Startup Community in Colorado and Beyond," *Colorado Sun*, December 4, 2018, https://coloradosun. com/2018/12/04/give-first-techstars-colorado-gives-entrepreneurs-startups/.

giving first, because it's the right thing to do and they want to support others.

This ethos can only spread when leaders set the right example. They understand that if they want people to give first, they need to do so themselves. They are constantly making introductions, helping young entrepreneurs out, and generally acting as a resource to others in the community.

Younger entrepreneurs pick up on this, and slowly learn that being selfless can benefit them in building a successful business and having fun too!

In addition to living this culture, leaders setting the pace intentionally strive to reward others who do the same. They seek out others who are behaving in a selfless, giving way and recognize them for their efforts. Most communities celebrate their most successful entrepreneurs, *but shifting culture requires celebrating those who live that culture.*

In our work in Upstate New York, we use the UVC Annual Conference and Awards as an opportunity to do this explicitly. We encourage community members to nominate people they see who are connecting and engaging with the community, and we focus the awards on encouraging the actions that we know support the long-term health of the culture. This not only helps those who deserve recognition to be celebrated, but also reinforces the values we want to imbue in the community at large.

UVC's annual Upstate Unleashed Conference (visit UVC.org/upstate-unleashed) draws about five hundred innovation economy leaders from over the entire Upstate New York region for a combination of ecosystem programming, interaction opportunities with peer leaders, and awards recognizing those individuals making their mark for ecosystem-building contributions. Our 2019 award categories included:

- **Community Catalyst**—Individuals who organize programs to bring together diverse startup ecosystem players in a local community.
- **David M. Ahlers Master Ecosystem Builder**—Someone who has invested a significant amount of time and energy into creating an impact across entrepreneurial communities.
- **Deal of the Year**—For a company whose exit created wealth for investors and founders/employees, as well as making the company a stronger contributor to the local economy.

We make similar efforts, on a smaller scale, through our online communications, where we highlight how those who have given great referrals have served the community, and consistently remind our followers that sharing their relationships is an important part of how they can help local companies.

PRIVATE REFERRAL NETWORK

More than anything else, creating a culture of giving is going to be the best path to increasing referrals by trusted sources within our community. However, there are other, more tactical solutions that can help as well. One such tactic is to create a private referral network, building trust among members based on admission to the group. These networks will never replace the right culture, but they can do a lot to supplement it.

The goal of a private referral network is to bring together a group of people with influence and relationships, and create an environment that encourages referrals. For example, creating a seed capital fund where investors meet on a regular basis is likely to create referrals among them, based on the types of companies they are interacting with.

These types of networks are common amongst investors, but the same principle holds in other circles. In Upstate New York, we created the UNY50 (visit UVC.org/UNY50), a group of individuals we recognize as doing the most to build the startup ecosystem in our region. We have a governance process to nominate and approve the group members exclusively, then point some resources toward getting members introduced to each other in ways that allow for easy communication and interaction, even across geographies.

This is where culture comes back into play. Naturally, the trust was high because the group was exclusive, but we also had the intentionality to choose people with a give first mentality and reinforce that mindset in all of our communications and group interactions. With those pieces in place, the high-quality referrals flowed—especially once we installed some platform and process that helped scale up the volume and quality of the interactions between members of the group.

DOUBLE OPT-IN REFERRALS

As we stoke up the number of referrals connecting entrepreneurs to highly influential people (whom we'll discuss in chapter 6) with resources inside their personal networks, we can also help set the example for how to increase the effectiveness of our referral approach.

Beyond the basics of having the two parties being connected getting sufficient context for why we think the referral is of value to both of them, we advocate the best practice approach of double opt in, confirming interest with both parties independently before making the connection.

For example, suppose an entrepreneur we know is building a product to be sold into the restaurant industry and we know someone who runs a restaurant or is an executive in a large hospitality company. Instead of lobbing an email over the transom, blindly connecting the parties because we think it's a great fit, we take the time to speak first with the entrepreneur to describe why we think the restaurateur or corporate exec is a good fit. We then do the same for HIPs we want to connect to the entrepreneur.

Doing that separately before bringing the parties together further builds our credibility with both parties in the interaction. There are numerous reasons from the perspective of either party that would cause the referral not to be timely or appropriate—we're then worse off if we fell into that trap of making a referral, and the trusted sources we're counting on responding now have to dig themselves out of a quagmire they didn't want to enter.

With the permission of both parties, our email or introduction now paves the way for a referral adding value to both parties, as they've each confirmed their interest and are queued up to interact.

FOSTERING THE RIGHT CULTURE IS ACCOMPLISHED ONE RELATIONSHIP AT A TIME

Actions like scaling up the volume and quality of creative collisions and referrals by trusted source allow a community to foster more entrepreneurial connections, build more successful companies, and, thus, create more good jobs. Yet when some experienced entrepreneurs hear about these goals, their first reaction is intimidation. Changing a community's culture is a big goal, and it seems difficult to imagine it's something we could do in our spare time.

The fortunate news is that, like many societal changes, creating a job-generating culture happens in small steps. There is no centralized authority that can magically nudge such a culture into existence. When governments attempt to make such sweeping changes, they miss the mark: their attempts aren't led by entrepreneurs, they can't help but have a constituency focus, and they don't understand the real needs of entrepreneurs.

When individual entrepreneurs strive to make these changes, a series of small acts of leadership can add up to something much greater than the sum of the parts. There's no one activity that is going to create a community. No one organization is going to make the difference in making a city startup-friendly. It takes many different efforts from many different people, all working in the same direction, even if they aren't entirely coordinated.

Most of the greatest movements in history began this way, from the bottom up, with individuals engaging in small acts of leadership. Movements don't begin as movements. Rather, they begin as a series of little things, individual decisions pointed in the same direction. Eventually, they gather enough momentum for others to latch onto. The best thing we can do is not worry about the movement and instead focus on doing our small part effectively.

In the long term, this requires balancing two different ways of thinking: moving quickly to build from the ground up without waiting for permission, and thinking about scale in order to ensure that things are moving in the right direction. Fortunately, who better than entrepreneurs to balance these competing mindsets?

To succeed in the early stages of this new movement, entrepreneurs have a bias toward action. Understanding that starting a recurring event is the highest-value thing they can do to serve their community, many entrepreneurs will leap into action, breaking through challenges and barriers to make such a program a reality.

As things progress, many entrepreneurs are able to harness the lessons they've learned, leading through scale. They tend to be quick to galvanize others to support their mission, define opportunities for others to support the movement, and direct the ship toward the larger goal of creating more good jobs. By acting as leaders within the movement, they unleash the power of those who aren't as self-guided to contribute effectively.

SUPPORTING DIVERSITY REQUIRES PROACTIVE EFFORT AND APPLYING A DIFFERENT LENS

Flash points that gave rise to 2020's social justice movement brought heightened awareness to me and many others about institutional bias in our society that too many of us with privilege may have been blind to.

No matter how good my intentions, that raised awareness made me realize I wasn't doing enough to be proactive in seeking out opportunities to help minority entrepreneurs. More importantly, I was applying the wrong lens in examining opportunities I had where black and minority entrepreneurs accomplished much with limited resources but had not yet achieved the level of customer traction on par with other seed-stage investment deals coming into my view. Revenue traction is an easy and objective metric to settle into. But as any seasoned startup investor will acknowledge, grit of the entrepreneur is harder to gauge but matters even more than revenue growth that followed after capital was deployed.

Brad Feld's post "Thoughts on Sourcing Black Companies and Entrepreneurs"[11] presents a fist to the forehead kind of aha that helped me evolve to a different lens in seeking and examining opportunities presented by minority entrepreneurs. Not only in my own investing, but also in helping me work these themes into conversations with others across my ecosystem stream so I can prod as many leaders as I can along these same lines.

11   Brad Feld, "Thoughts on Sourcing Black Companies and Entrepreneurs," *Feld Thoughts*, July 20, 2020, https://feld.com/archives/2020/07/thoughts-on-sourcing-black-companies-and-entrepreneurs.html.

THOUGHTS ON SOURCING BLACK
COMPANIES AND ENTREPRENEURS
BY BRAD FELD ON JULY 20, 2020, 01:15 PM

I recently was in an email thread where a Black founder had a powerful and clear response to the question from one of her corporate partners. The question was:

How can our (the corporate partner's) team better support diversity in our work, particularly in our sourcing, diligence, and onboarding efforts?

The entrepreneur responded with a long explanation that was a brilliant and extremely helpful perspective for me. It follows.

I think one of my core experiences, and a truth that we all have to grapple with, is that programs like yours should be thought of like higher education in 1960, or getting into a NYC Specialized High School today.

Were there no Black students at Harvard because Black people aren't brilliant? No.

There were no Black students at Harvard because you have to get a certain score on the SAT to get in.

People who score well on the SAT either:

1. Come from amazing school districts with a plethora of funding and the ability to prepare students adequately for the test.
2. Come from families that can afford expensive SAT prep.
3. Come from communities that have an infrastructure that supports robust SAT prep.

Because of institutional racism in our society, Black people:

1. Have school systems with a lower tax basis and insufficient resources.
2. Make less than half what whites do in many cities and don't have the resources to sign up for SAT prep.
3. Have had our communities and families decimated through mass incarceration and other racist policies.

If we juxtapose that analogy with startups, your team will need to ask itself what criteria you're using for startups.

Black entrepreneurs have to find a way/make a way/invent a way to launch businesses with two arms tied behind our backs because we don't get the same funding as our white counterparts.

So I have raised $2.5MM and have to compete with companies who have raised $25m and $70m respectively.

And yet, I'm constantly asked, "What's your traction?" which is similar to "What's your SAT score?"

We know that as a society, we are starving Black businesses for capital, and yet we expect them to hit the same milestone markers as businesses that have a plethora of capital. It's like not feeding a cow yet expecting them to produce milk. It's literally madness and maddening.

Thinking about your sourcing of Black companies is going to be a far more complex question than "Who do we call to find the amazing Black companies?" It's going to be "How do we change our lens so we can see the amazing Black companies?" followed by "Once we bring them into our ecosystem, how do we support their journey in meaningful ways that can help to level the playing field = e.g. get them capital or get them revenue?"

Maybe we should stop asking "What's your SAT score?" and instead ask, "Wow. How on earth did you maintain a 3.7 GPA, and cook for your little brother and sister every night because your mom had 2 jobs, and get an A in calculus without a high-paid tutor, and work a full-time summer job at Key Food while taking a class to teach you how to code at night? That's a lot of grit!"

Maybe we're measuring the wrong things in our entrepreneurial society, just as we've measured the wrong things in our larger society. Maybe we all need to start talking about grit instead of metrics that can only be achieved with money, and then make sure all entrepreneurs get the funding required to achieve equivalent metrics.

DEALING WITH SKEPTICS

Of course, leadership isn't always easy. In my experience, people will often assume the worst and be skeptical about your desire to create a movement. *What's in it for you? What are you trying to gain from all this?*

The best way to handle these concerns is to be completely transparent and genuine. Live the culture you are trying to create: be consistent in supporting the community; don't be transactional, looking for something in return; and, most importantly, be clear on your vision for the community.

Many people are embarrassed to voice their largest goals, fearing that others will laugh them off. The entrepreneurs who have succeeded most in creating these cultures have done the opposite—sharing their vision and their belief in the community, expressing that they are in it for the long term and serving as a beacon for others.

Eventually, from the efforts of just a few, momentum can start building for others to follow the example. As the community grows, it will need to have some intentional focus around ongoing communications, whether that involves a newsletter, a shared job posting, curated directories, or any number of other opportunities.

Meeting in the real world is a crucial first step to any community, but ongoing communication keeps members engaged and reinforces core principles of our ecosystem culture. For example, in Upstate New York, we decided in 2014 that we needed to double down on our communications efforts. We started to send email newsletters more consistently and began to take our social media presence more seriously. These efforts allowed those who attended events to stay engaged and also led to us bringing new folks into the fold.

There are hundreds of things we can do to grow and scale a job-generating community, but it doesn't need to start as a complicated undertaking. The work begins, simply, with entrepreneurs taking action to bring people together consistently, with an emphasis on openness, connecting people to help by giving first, and having fun by doing so with others who share these values.

SUMMARY

- To promote support within an entrepreneurial community, our most productive effort is to scale up the volume and quality of both creative collisions and referrals by trusted source.
- To generate more creative collisions, host recurring events that are open to the entire community and bring different facets of the startup ecosystem together.
- To generate more referrals by trusted source, we must change the culture. This is difficult, but it starts with leaders showing by example by giving first (without expectation of getting a return) and proactively seeking out entrepreneurs to help.
- Bringing public visibility to ecosystem builders who are demonstrating "give first" in helping entrepreneurs is another path to build high-impact referrals and get more people engaged.
- Without a proactive effort, you may miss spotting capable minority entrepreneurs with significant potential. The grit of the entrepreneur can be harder to measure than revenue traction, but examining this is worth the effort in bringing the value of diversity, as you raise up the entire community.
- Leading by example and repeating the core principles of the ecosystem are the two most important steps toward changing a community's culture—one relationship at a time.

CHAPTER 5

THE MAGNET CITY ETHOS

Culture eats strategy for breakfast.
—PETER DRUCKER

In our business or community, we can strategize as much as we'd like, but unless we create a culture that encourages the right behaviors, none of it matters.

As the CEO of TriNet, I came to understand the importance of company culture. Not by voicing lofty phrases, but by developing self-reinforcing mechanisms in which everyone on the team could be holding each other accountable to a shared set of core values woven into our building a company culture that people understood. Jim Collins helped me launch that process with inspiration from his classic book *Built to Last* and several other pieces he wrote on this theme.[12] Over years of deep discussions and experimentation, we distilled TriNet's beliefs into five core values, which we referred to by the acronym POISE—personal growth, orientation to the future, integrity, service, and entrepreneurial spirit.

---

12   Jim Collins, "Aligning Actions and Values," June 2000, https://www.jimcollins.com/article_topics/articles/aligning-action.html.

We didn't just write out these values. We lived them. We used them to screen candidates, celebrate success, communicate what's important, and fire people who didn't align. These values defined who we were as a company, and this clear definition allowed our company to achieve tremendous results. When a culture permeates a group or organization, it allows the members of that group to align in making good decisions, even without direct supervision or intervention from leaders.

Culture is what people do when nobody is watching, and when you're trying to create change in a community (rather than a company), nobody is watching most of the time.

Studying the cultures of successful entrepreneurial communities like Silicon Valley, Boulder, and Austin, I was struck by many of the underlying similarities. In creating more successful entrepreneurial communities, it's important for us to take lessons from what's worked.

WALKING THE TALK OF STARTUP COMMUNITIES

Brad Feld's insightful book *Startup Communities* is the best window into how this talk of values was walked into action with very clear outcomes fostering the build-out of what today is a true Magnet City: Boulder, Colorado. I'm not alone in crediting Brad as a major force propelling Boulder's incredible climb to become a destination startup hub, best evidenced by the city's ranking third in the United States on the metric of venture capital per capita (trailing only San Francisco and San Jose).

I had the good fortune of knowing Brad well before he moved to Boulder in 1995, as we collaborated for a few years on a Kauffman Foundation advisory board aimed at growing the then nascent Young Entrepreneurs' Organization (today known as Entrepreneurs' Organization, as too many of us no longer qualify as young!).

At the time Brad relocated, TriNet's customer base was 100 percent focused on emerging tech. Our market footprint then covered only the established startup hubs in Northern and Southern California, New York City, Boston, and the Northern Virginia DC metroplex. While Boulder had so little startup activity that it did not even register as a target market for TriNet, my experience in working with Brad while he was investing and helping others build companies in the Boston area led me to believe his relocation to a smaller community would inject leadership and vision that would in turn create enough opportunity to support a new TriNet office.

So I had a ringside seat viewing and participating in community-building efforts Brad led in finding other leaders who shared his passion for making an open, give first culture take root as the foundation for building a highly effective startup community.

Startup Communities outlines Brad's Boulder Thesis, which aligns deeply with the message of this book. This chapter is drawn heavily from the work Brad has done to distill the ideal entrepreneurial community culture, with some additions based on UVC's effort in Upstate New York.

Five traits are remarkably consistent across the leaders of successful entrepreneurially led communities, and it's our job to ingrain these traits in the cultures of our communities as well.

- Entrepreneurs are visible and accessible.
- Leaders and community members are open to new ideas.

- The community is inclusive rather than exclusive.
- Leaders give first.
- Entrepreneurs have a desire to improve their community.

These are the individual and community traits that I observe Talent Exporting Cities too often overlook as they attempt to grow entrepreneurial activity. In this chapter, I'll talk about each of these traits, why they're important, and what it looks like to build a community around them.

TRAIT #1: A GOOD CULTURE MAKES SUCCESSFUL ENTREPRENEURS VISIBLE AND ACCESSIBLE

In Silicon Valley, Boulder, or Austin, you can walk into any public event for entrepreneurs and be confident that you'll have the opportunity to connect with experienced entrepreneurs and community business leaders face-to-face. Any interested young entrepreneur can identify the successful entrepreneurs in the community and get in touch with them for the right reason.

In Talent Exporting Cities, entrepreneurs are more likely to spend inordinate amounts of time in their office—focused on *only* their business—without engaging in the broader community. Even if their company is growing, the rookie entrepreneurs who could be learning and taking inspiration from those further down the path don't have the exposure to see how others could be helping them with their own company-building effort.

Building a culture where successful entrepreneurs carve out slices of time to attend community events and activities, and actually talk to people, is the crucial first step to creating a culture that supports innovation economy companies.

To begin to build this culture, our job as leaders is to draw successful entrepreneurs out of hiding and into the public sphere. We'll get into specific tactics throughout the rest of this book, but whether the effort is to create an angel investment fund, host regular startup events, or organize opportunities for entrepreneurs to share their stories, the important thing is to build a culture in which entrepreneurs and leaders with business success are expected to interact with the newbie entrepreneurs.

The lesson to instill in the seasoned entrepreneurs is how these interactions are aligned with their personal and professional interests as they give back, including the broader rewards that come with a flourishing entrepreneurial community.

This isn't just a lesson for veterans, though. Even new entrepreneurs have a tendency to keep their heads down, completely absorbed in their work. Especially for those trying to develop a new product, it's easy to get sucked into the task at hand and never venture into the broader community. They forget to increase their knowledge and, more importantly, build relationships. Part of the culture we try to build involves an ongoing stream of reminders to new entrepreneurs that venturing out to foster new relationships is an important part of their journey that will help increase the odds of building a successful company.

I saw this problem firsthand in Upstate New York. When I moved back here, we had an incredible quantity of successful entrepreneurial talent and experience, but individuals weren't accessible because they didn't know how to find each other. In the Hudson Valley, I met an entrepreneur named Kale Kaposhilin who fit this mold exactly: his business was growing, but rarely visible to others. His low profile was a missed opportunity for both his company and the community.

UVC engaged in a dialogue to help Kale explore his interests and how we might help support him in a community-building effort. Kale settled on launching a tech meetup group, embracing principles like those outlined in this chapter. He organized it, publicized it, and executed it beautifully. Lo and behold, among the event's attendees were hundreds of neighboring entrepreneurs whom Kale never even knew existed.

By creating an opportunity to bring people together in the right structured format—and then marketing it effectively (including help from UVC channels), Kale drew out people who had previously been stuck working in their homes and small offices. It doesn't take too many events where people are regularly bumping into each other with creative collisions like this before relationships form that become the basis for spreading the startup community culture and attracting even more new people into the fold.

TRAIT #2: A GOOD CULTURE IS OPEN TO NEW IDEAS

Successful entrepreneurial communities are populated by people who don't automatically reject ideas just because they've never heard them before. Silicon Valley is a paragon of this trait.

By contrast, in most Talent Exporting Cities, the first instinct for most executives (and, to be honest, most people) is to be *critical* of new ideas. Even successful entrepreneurs in Upstate New York can be predisposed to belittling new ideas. I've seen startup founders explain their business model to an experienced entrepreneur and heard the veteran respond, "Listen, that's just not how business is done. Here are five reasons why your startup will fail..."

Even if they aren't so explicit, successful founders in Talent Exporting Cities too often seem to have closed-minded dialogues going on in their heads. Because they live in an area that isn't as flush with innovative companies and skyrocketing growth, the vets can too easily fall into the trap of assuming that the way they succeeded with their business, and the way they understand the world to work, is the only way for other entrepreneurs to forge a path to success in the future.

On the other end of the spectrum is the Magnet City ethos. In thriving communities filled with innovation economy companies, people approach new ideas—even ideas that sound ill-conceived at first—as something interesting to explore.

When we first started TriNet, nobody understood the nature of what we did. We were asking people to outsource their HR. In those days, you couldn't put *HR* and *outsourcing* in the same sentence and expect anything less than confused silence. But in the Bay Area, the reactions were different. Silicon Valley founders stayed open-minded, thought about the HR problems they were seeking to solve, and didn't brush the idea off for not fitting their mold. Open-mindedness like that bolstered my own self-confidence and helped me secure the introductions needed to get the business off the ground.

Culture starts with how the leaders act, so the way we respond to new ideas is incredibly impactful. Rather than reflexively rejecting an idea that I don't understand, I try to explicitly state what I don't understand and talk about it. Being curious and considering new processes, models, markets, approaches, and technologies is what's fun about interacting in the space of the newer industries. Showing that enthusiasm inspires others to do the same.

TRAIT #3: A GOOD CULTURE IS INCLUSIVE AND WELCOMING

In TriNet's early days, I was going from event to event pitching this new concept of outsourced HR, and I was impressed by how Silicon Valley founders stayed open-minded to the idea. What impressed me even more was how inclusive and welcoming many people were, even though I wasn't a techie or fully plugged into the Silicon Valley scene yet.

I was a first-time entrepreneur selling a product that no one had ever heard of before, and yet the Silicon Valley community welcomed me with open arms. People I met included me in their community, often inviting me to other events or introducing me to a friend who might need our services.

Compared to Silicon Valley, people in Talent Exporting Cities can have too strong a focus on their constituency. In other words, leaders of companies and organizations (and then the people they lead) can drift into the mindset of showing affinity and openness only to the small subgroup rather than the community at large. Small-market entrepreneurial events tend to limit their participants based on geography or industry classification. Either way, they come up with some definition of their constituency, and everything becomes focused on that group. These distinctions are not only useless, they're counterproductive.

A strong culture encourages people of diverse backgrounds to join and cross-pollinate ideas, regardless of their so-called constituency. In fact, they don't even see themselves as separate groups. Yes, the people in successful entrepreneurial communities may identify with their particular interests—and are more likely to attend events that cater to those interests—but they do not exclude others from attending. Whether it's a tech event or an HR event, they tell the world: *Whoever is interested is welcome.*

As we defined our community's culture, we put an added focus on creating a nonterritorial community where everyone is welcome. We never know where the best connections and ideas will come from.

TRAIT #4: A GOOD CULTURE ENCOURAGES PEOPLE TO GIVE FIRST

Give and Take author Adam Grant's data shows that the most successful people in the world of business are givers. This mentality applies beyond the world of business; givers who can provide value for others first are the most successful people in any field.

In *Startup Communities*, Brad Feld referred to "Give before you get" as one of his personal beliefs underlying how he approached numerous interactions with startup ecosystem people. With him visibly leading by example, over time this spread through the Boulder startup culture, eventually morphing into Techstars' #GiveFirst—which we, and many other startup ecosystem builders, have adopted as a key mantra.

When a culture adopts a give first mentality, the results can be incredible. This shift in focus allows everyone to give selflessly, without worrying about getting their piece. The cumulative effects of this shift improve everyone's opportunities.

For this shift to work, the giving cannot be transactional. There are too many business events where everyone "gives" by transactionally asking each other for favors. This is taking disguised as giving. In the most successful entrepreneurial cultures, people give first without any expectation of receiving something in return.

What's amazing about giving without expectation of return is that the more you give, the more you end up getting, in ways that you couldn't have expected or imagined. If you act from that selfless place, you'll reap the benefits in your own life, your business, and the community at large.

Johnny LeHane of the Hudson Valley Startup Fund is a great example of someone who gives first. When we first met, Johnny wasn't an investor but an entrepreneur running his company. After some coaxing, he ended up leading the effort to set up a seed capital fund (a strategy we'll discuss in the next chapter). He put in the work to form a team for launching a successful fund, thereby helping area startups find a precious source of early-stage capital not previously available. In the end, he got his effort back in spades by making valuable connections in the community beneficial to him beyond the goal of creating the seed fund.

As a result of putting the fund together, he's transformed how he looks at his own business and met new people who helped him. What made Johnny successful was that his actions were not motivated by money (although he'll end up getting a decent return from investing in the seed fund) but instead by a desire to improve his community.

Again, this behavior and culture starts with leaders. To spread a give first culture, embody a give first mentality. Even if you don't know what the payoff will be, know that the community is stronger if you set the standard of consistently giving without any expectation of return.

In places like Silicon Valley, where giving first is the norm, everyone sees the positive effects and creates a virtuous cycle. This can be a difficult shift in communities that aren't used to operating this way. Never underestimate the value of leading the way by living the example of giving first.

TRAIT #5: A GOOD CULTURE IS BASED ON AN EXPLICIT DESIRE TO IMPROVE THE COMMUNITY

People commonly assume that everyone wants to improve their community, but when that goal isn't discussed explicitly, assumptions can lead to misalignment. With different definitions of what is necessary to work toward, different time horizons, and different resources, a coordinated effort is unlikely. To make things worse, many entrepreneurs naturally think of a strong community as a fortunate byproduct of doing other things right, not as a goal in and of itself.

By explicitly discussing the goal of improving the community by helping create more innovation economy companies, we are able to align resources to move toward that goal.

This is especially important because the changes we're discussing in this book don't happen overnight. In fact, the real opportunities won't materialize in a year, or even two or three. For people who want to see quick results (this includes the government, which we'll talk about in a later chapter), such an extended time horizon is challenging. According to Brad Feld, to create a thriving startup community, you should be assuming a twenty-year time horizon. That seems about right to me—especially when I realize where we are today in Upstate New York and the progress we have made ten years after starting with zero network across our broad geography.

To create a long-term focus on improving the community in our culture, we must talk about the shifts that are happening on a community level. We need to engage entrepreneurs in the project of building a thriving community filled with innovation economy companies, not just reaching a particular organization's annual goal or targets.

Once people see how smaller actions and results are stepping stones to a transformed community over the coming decades, each contributor in the network has a better chance to align their actions toward outcomes that feed into a collective cultural change that transforms the overall community.

HOW TO CREATE A CULTURE

You may see a pattern in these cultural values. In most cases, cultural change starts with our own behavior and cascades out to the people who follow us.

This is intentional, and it's a good thing. Acronyms like TriNet's POISE are useful, but they are meaningless unless they are lived. The most effective cultural changes always start with leading by example.

This has certainly been the case in Boulder. Brad Feld practices the behaviors that he advocates as crucial to the community's growth. He always gives first, thinks long term, and embodies the traits that he wants to see in the rest of the community. Importantly, he hangs out with others who embrace these values, and you won't see him spending time with those on the opposite end of the spectrum.

If we live our mission—clearly communicating it as we do— we'll inspire like-minded leaders who believe in building an entrepreneurially friendly culture. They'll want to share it, repeat it, live it, and reward it, and soon they'll be behaving in a way that benefits the whole community.

When I coach and mentor entrepreneurs on their journey to create successful companies that boost their community, I work in ways that reinforce values I've discussed in this chapter: be visible and accessible, stay open-minded to new ideas, be inclusive and welcoming, give first, and explicitly aim to improve our community. But the most important gift I can give is enacting those values in my own community efforts and becoming an example that others can model, which I hope in turn inspires people around them to do the same.

Creating a community culture is different from creating a company culture. In a single company, we have the ability to hold people accountable to the company's values, but nobody in our community will be accountable to us. We can't explicitly eject companies or people from the larger community for failing to line up with our values (though, as with any system, a strong culture will result in sidelining those who are running contrary to the accepted social norms the group shares).

As Brad propagated the pay-it-forward ethos in Boulder, there were no explicit incentives for others to do so. He simply gave without expecting anything in return and highlighted the philosophy in his writing, public speaking, and numerous personal interactions. His example inspired others.

Another major tool we have to amp up culture reinforcement is giving broader visibility to the right examples through an ongoing communications stream. This is a key piece of the UVC strategy to have a constantly growing communications channel that sends reinforcing messages across our newsletters, blog posts, social media, and events.

Although it's not easily measured, we believe our culture is the most important resource for growing innovation economy companies in our communities. Culture dictates the way people default to acting, and if we can create the right behavioral norms, people will serve each other and foster more innovation economy companies, even without our personal involvement.

This is why culture is so powerful. When the norms in a community change, the community itself changes, and the results are more dramatic than what any one person could achieve on their own.

THE ROAD AHEAD

In part 1 of this book, we discussed why creating more good jobs is crucial to help our struggling cities survive, and why this starts with creating a culture that helps entrepreneurs thrive. We explored the economics behind this reality, the types of businesses that lead to the most overall job growth, and the challenges faced by Talent Exporting Cities.

In part 2, we've looked at the high-level view of how to create the environment of a job-generating community. We examined how new entrepreneurs succeed, how communities can support them in getting connected to the resources they need, and the type of culture that's needed to cultivate this environment.

Now, we are ready for part 3. Each of the remaining chapters focuses on an individual type of stakeholder in the community—highly influential people, investors with private capital, educational institutions, nonprofits, government entities, and finally, us as leaders—explaining what role each of these stakeholders can play in creating an entrepreneurial community filled with innovation economy jobs.

SUMMARY

- Culture is crucially important to the success of a community. Brad Feld's two-decades-plus of walking the talk in how to shape startup ecosystem culture is profiled in his book *Startup Communities*—a great resource for local leaders wanting to drive change.
- The Magnet City ethos has five traits: make successful entrepreneurs visible and accessible, be open to new ideas, be inclusive and welcoming, encourage all to give first, and be explicit that the goal for all this is based on the desire to improve the community.
- Changing the culture of a community is difficult, because members of the community aren't accountable to you (and you can't fire them!). The best tool you have is the ability to lead by example and look for ways to join with others who are doing the same.
- Providing broader visibility to concrete examples of leaders in our community who are living the give first mantra can be a worthwhile content stream for digital communication channels.

PART 3

KEY PARTNERS

CHAPTER 6

ENGAGING HIGHLY INFLUENTIAL PEOPLE

HOW TO GET VIPS TO HELP JUMPSTART YOUR COMMUNITY

You can make more friends in two months by becoming interested in other people than you can in two years by trying to get other people interested in you.

—DALE CARNEGIE

In the Western world, and especially in America, we love the story of the self-made man or woman. We see ending slavery as the work of Lincoln, Indian independence as a result of Gandhi, and building Apple as a Herculean effort by Steve Jobs.

The reality, of course, is far more subtle and complicated than that. Nothing of significance is achieved solely by the efforts of a single individual. As innovation expert Jeff Havens wrote, "In the history of our species, everyone who has ever accomplished anything has had parents or guardians who cared for them; educators, mentors, and role models who taught them essential skills; friends, supporters, and other interested parties who provided moral or intellectual or financial support; and countless partners who helped them build, tweak, promote, modify, expand, establish, and grow whatever it is that they ended up doing."[13]

No matter how grand our own ambitions or how compelling our message might be, none of us by ourselves can effect true transformation on our own. If we are to create change in our community, we need to engage and grow legions of others who share in our vision for what might be possible.

WHY GET HIGHLY INFLUENTIAL PEOPLE ON BOARD?

In order to create the movement we've been discussing over the past few chapters, the first order of business is to attract the right people to support the cause. Getting HIPs on board as early adopters in your community can be the rocket fuel that turns your plan into a movement.

These HIPs can take many forms and can help in any number of ways. They can contribute to your efforts directly, whether through their time, their talent, or their treasure. They can provide social proof, publicly endorsing your efforts as legitimate and mobilizing their personal network to support the cause. This creates an exponential force, as one HIP brings other HIPs into the fold.

At the top of the list of HIPs to target are other entrepreneurs. They have the greatest wealth of experience when it comes to building businesses and creating jobs. More importantly, entrepreneurs appreciate how difficult the journey of building

---

13 Jeff Havens, "4 Reasons You Shouldn't Try to Do Everything Yourself," *Fast Company*, May 1, 2014, https://www.fastcompany.com/3029889/4-reasons-you-shouldnt-try-to-do-everything-yourself.

something new is, and are often the first to support when they see someone doing something new and ambitious.

In addition, cast a net to look at others already in leadership roles within your community: government, community groups, or business. Successful people in leadership roles are likely to be good communicators and have a following of their own.

The right people can help with not just their time and energy, but also their most valuable asset: their willingness to engage their network for the cause. Granted, everyone has a network of some kind, but those who have achieved success as leaders are likely to have broader networks that allow them to have an outsized impact in the community.

Those who fit the profile of connectors have demonstrated the ability to bring other people into your movement at a rapid pace. Since people are the essential ingredient, connectors are extraordinarily powerful people to have on your side.

WHAT ABOUT OTHERS WHO AREN'T YET RECOGNIZED AS HIPS?

Of course, your movement isn't going to be made up entirely of successful entrepreneurs and community leaders. Making change requires a team, and no team is made up entirely of leaders.

Volunteers who care about the mission and are willing to help are invaluable to getting things done, especially for making events come to life on an ongoing basis. Sometimes energetic volunteers are early in their careers and ready to dive in and roll up their sleeves.

They don't have a track record, but they can and will contribute time and talent, which is incredibly valuable.

But don't overlook others, including those whose first impression might not exude energy or passion, as they may not yet be in the right setting to flourish to their own potential.

Volunteers can help with hundreds of potential activities: organizing or supporting events, contributing content, participating in outreach, or doing any other tasks that help advance the cause.

When someone asks me how they might help, I've found it best to have a little dialogue about their interests and strengths, followed by querying them on their ideas to plug in. And if that doesn't yield anything suitable, then share a few possible ideas to get feedback on.

The best way I've found to move that person from talker to doer involves my thinking fast enough about coming up with an assignment of some kind that aligns with their interest but requires some level of effort on their part to complete and report back on. It might be just a small effort, but just going through the process helps sort out who is truly interested in contributing.

The most important factor in whether a volunteer can succeed in making an impact is that they have a bias for action. If a volunteer has the ability to take action and deliver results, no matter how small, you can usually be confident that they will add value to the community.

WHERE DO I FIND HIGHLY INFLUENTIAL PEOPLE?

When new job creators begin the search for highly influential people, they often face a strange paradox. On the one hand, the goal of transforming a community might seem overwhelming.

There may be thousands of successful people in their community and no clear path to start. For others, the same task looks like a problem of scarcity. Especially in smaller towns, there seems to be a shortage of people who meet your criteria, and finding the right HIPs can feel hopeless.

To solve this paradox, we want to both focus and expand our search. We'll focus by defining exactly who the best HIPs are locally, and then find pathways to connect with them. Expanding beyond the local community follows the same approach: Who are the HIPs in our region or otherwise connected to the community and how can we get connected to them?

Let's start with a definition: the most highly influential people are those who are successful, give first, and have credibility in the local community.

What do we mean by successful? Entrepreneurs who have built businesses are of the highest value. What you are looking for is evidence that they have the knowledge, expertise, and network to guide others in your community in a strong direction.

We look for successful companies or organizations in our area and explore who started them, who are the high-up executives, and who has invested time and/or money in community-building or private companies beyond their own. We are always delighted to find there are many fascinating companies, and individuals come out of the woodwork that (until we sought them out) we didn't know were there.

What do we mean by giving first? We find that the strongest communities are built around people who freely give value without asking for or expecting to get something in return. It is impossible to build a movement surrounded by those who are always looking to get their piece of the pie in anything they are involved with.

In his iconic book *Give and Take*, Wharton professor Adam Grant explains that people tend to fall into three groups: givers, matchers, and takers. Givers actively look for ways to be helpful and give to others. Matchers play tit-for-tat transactional games. They will reciprocate and also expect reciprocity for what they give. Takers focus on getting as much as possible from others. As you search for highly influential people, especially early on in your movement, it's crucial to find those who are givers to help lead the charge.

Some sure signs of this is that they give of themselves regularly. Look for those who donate time or money generously, who are involved in mentoring and improving the community, who are known as connectors, and those who—despite their success—continue to make themselves visible and accessible to others.

What do we mean by having credibility with the local community? One of the most important roles these highly influential people will play is to continue to bring more people into the fold. Those who are known and respected within your community have the ability to do this, both through their networks and also through the reputational advantage you receive by working with them.

Look for local leaders who are talked about consistently in the local media and discussed by your early HIPs. You'll likely hear the same names coming up over and over again. They are not limited to successful entrepreneurs, and these are the people who can have the biggest impact on your movement.

I like to call these particular people HIP magnets. With only a few magnets on your side, you'll be off to a great start to credibly attract and connect with others to get your movement off the launchpad.

Mohawk Valley Community College president Randy Van-Wagoner is an example of someone in my community who fits these criteria. When I met him in about 2012, he'd already built an amazing reputation because of his high integrity and get-things-done attitude. People in the community understand that even as an academic, he is one of the smartest and most influential businesspeople in Upstate's Utica/Rome area. Randy's word is a seal of approval in our community. CEOs and other successful businesspeople listen to him and say, "If Randy says it's the real deal, then it's the real deal."

He doesn't enjoy that credibility simply because of his position, but because of the success he's had in helping others. They respect him as a person, not as a title, and that respect allows him to make connections and open doors for our movement that wouldn't be possible without his help.

EXPANDING THE SEARCH FOR HIGHLY INFLUENTIAL PEOPLE

With the above criteria, you likely will be surprised by the number of highly influential people who are somewhere within your community. However, as your movement grows and your needs expand, you will see gaps in the support your local community can provide.

Upstate Venture Connect serves seven metro areas, some of which are populated by more than a million people. Even in a million-plus person metro area, the perfect resource for a particular startup may be there but not be visible or accessible for us to reach them.

Fortunately, HIP recruiting can and should extend far beyond your local area. The first way to expand your search is to open the doors to neighboring communities. When the entrepreneur with a limited network starts searching for a particular resource—whether a mentor with a specialized skillset, an introduction to companies in a particular industry, or a specific kind of funding—too often they lack reach to what's beyond their current visibility. The perfect resource might be available just one community over, but if there's no connectivity across neighboring areas, everyone misses out on the chance to help make things happen.

There's nothing malicious about entrepreneurs' insular tendencies. Most successful people don't even realize they have blinders on. They just focus on helping their own local community, as that's where they think they can leverage their current network. As a result, they miss broader opportunities that could support their community even further by going beyond their current boundaries and helping others who in turn will bring value back into the local community.

It's our job as ecosystem leaders to help others take these self-imposed blinders off. Set the example by exploring the surrounding region and building connections beyond your local community. Give first, and plug yourself into other local networks. Get to know the HIPs in your community. In return, plug them into your own network and create an opportunity for a constant flow of referrals by trusted sources among communities across a broader geography than a single community.

Innovation economy companies have specialized needs, so this branching out is crucial. In the Syracuse community, for example, if we have a cybersecurity company looking for help, there aren't a lot of resources and experts available to them locally. However, if they go just forty miles to the east, there are a bunch of cybersecurity resources in Utica/Rome. Likewise, forty miles west in Rochester, there are also a lot of software, telecom, and financial service resources. These situations are incredibly common, and focusing on our narrow community while ignoring the broader region means our local startups miss potentially life-changing opportunities to connect with resources next door.

Outsiders are often surprised to learn that, on a good day, it will take you two hours to drive from Marin County (just north of San Francisco) to San Jose, yet that's all considered the same community. We call it *the Bay Area*, which reinforces this idea. Because they think about their networks in broad, regional terms, people will make that two-hour drive for a networking event to meet the right people. In the rest of the country, people sometimes act like they need a passport to drive to a community forty minutes away.

I had the experience of meeting incredible highly influential people as I expanded my network regionally by seeking out creative collision opportunities.

One amazing guy is Richard Glaser, a financial advisor with Merrill Lynch's Rochester office. He's a former venture capitalist, so he understands emerging tech, and he works tirelessly to connect people—including community-building groups he created, like Roc Growth, which brings a curated group of the right people together in a fashion that drives growth of creative collisions on a recurring basis.

With every single person he meets, he asks them what they want to accomplish in the community and how he can help them. He has built a vast network of HIPs who would do anything for him because he does so much for them *without asking for anything in return*.

I knew from my first meeting with Richard he was an uberconnector of the highest order, but at that time his focus was almost exclusively on the Rochester community. As our relationship grew over time, he evolved his thinking to view the community as encompassing a larger region. He now advocates crossing both geographic and institutional boundaries and personally sets that example with all those he interacts with.

ENGAGING HIPS FROM A DISTANCE

Another productive path we've found to expand the search for highly influential people who can help is to think through who might have meaningful ties to the community even if they don't live there. These people might include those who grew up locally, attended an area college, or have family relations or some other connection to the area.

When a community lacks an innovation economy, the most talented people often leave for greater opportunities elsewhere. They may come back to visit friends and family, but their talents are being deployed elsewhere instead of at home. Fortunately, some of these HIPs are willing to help because they still care about their community.

So while Talent Exporting Cities sometimes bemoan the loss of these "expatriates," we find this pool well worth the energy to research, identify, and find pathways to connect to.

To identify these people, start by seeking successful alumni from colleges in your region. At UVC, we started making a list of people we'd love to have involved in our community who attended college in Upstate New York. We've found that some of these people are happy to support the part of the country where they spent four years—though we don't know which ones until we invest the time to get introduced and then nurture the relationship.

We pay especially close attention to successful entrepreneurs who leave the area but come back for startup events, as this shows interest in supporting the local community. For example, Bill Trenchard, partner at First Round Capital, grew up in the Upstate New York area, but now lives in Silicon Valley. He comes back every year for an event called Entrepreneurship at Cornell Celebration. I sought him out and informed him about Upstate Venture Connect's activities, and I strive to maintain an open dialogue. As a give first guy who is out there helping others, Bill opened up doors to us that led to other relationships helping our Upstate companies and growing the UVC network.

Just like the challenges involving anything in sales, one contact is not enough to nurture a relationship, so occasional touches to explore ways in which the UVC network can be deployed to help in his efforts at First Round are top of mind for me.

Keep your eyes out for the Bill Trenchards at your events. Even if highly influential people leave the area, they often still have roots there. They might return for family, to speak at alumni events at their alma mater, or to support local nonprofits. Recruit those people, bring them into your network, and show them just how much your community has changed since they left.

HIP EXTRAORDINAIRE JORDAN LEVY

For the Buffalo/Niagara community, Jordan Levy would be the textbook example of a highly influential person having outsized impact through investing his time, resources, and reputation to make things happen in building the local startup community.

Jordan built and exited multiple businesses (including public companies Ingram Micro and GameStop), then became a nationally prominent venture capitalist in New York City (serving as managing partner of Softbank Capital New York and Seed Capital Partners) while maintaining a presence in Buffalo, where he steadily chipped away toward a long-term vision of fostering a supportive environment for local tech companies.

Mentoring and investing in local entrepreneurs was the easy starting point, as both are in his wheelhouse as an uber-entrepreneur and professional investor. But seeking a larger impact beyond the entrepreneurs and companies he might personally interact with, Jordan built support with local businesspeople to become active in early-stage investing and also invested energy in influencing local political leaders about innovation economy issues and how they could help with resources and support.

After tiring of listening to people complain about the lack of a startup ecosystem, Jordan led the founding of Z80 Labs, a private capital-backed incubator for local tech companies and one of the first such facilities in Upstate New York. Jordan was instrumental in forging the path for the New York State government-led program 43 North (visit 43North.org) and also the nonprofit Launch New York, where he continues in the role of vice chairman (visit LaunchNY.org).

Jordan's super success as a tech entrepreneur and venture capitalist paved the way for his being able to open doors at any level. While he continues in a variety of investment roles, it is his leadership in putting his personal reputation on the line in constantly building new and committed relationships for the innovation economy community that sets the example for other leaders to follow.

HOW TO GET HIGHLY INFLUENTIAL PEOPLE INVOLVED

First, a warning: this isn't easy. Successful entrepreneurs and leaders are extraordinarily opportunity rich, and with so many high-quality demands on their time, it's hard for something they've not heard about before to stand out as worthy of their attention.

This is doubly true when people reach out and ask them to give money or commit to a major investment of time. For someone as busy as many successful entrepreneurs are, this is akin to mentioning interest in marriage to someone on the first date. Instead, I've found it best to take my time developing the relationship in smaller ways.

There are many ways to get highly influential people involved, but the key is to have a clear-cut, definable ask that they can agree to.

In Upstate New York, we created a venture accelerator called StartFast. Each summer, over the course of a twelve-week program, we've helped startups go from "garage-level" to being ready to raise money from investors. We launched StartFast on the premise that it was the perfect ask to bring to HIPs we wanted to engage, by asking them to be a listed mentor for the program. This was an easy task for them to say yes to.

Sometimes those mentors would make an on-site appearance at StartFast. Others came in on video teleconference or just served on standby so our program managers could match up a startup's need to a specific mentor on our roster.

Once an HIP is engaged, we've also found them to be receptive to other approaches outside of StartFast. The venture accelerator becomes an intake vehicle to get both local and distant HIPs into the network, but we then cultivate those relationships to help in other ways. We'll go more in depth on the StartFast program design, funding and evolution in Chapter 7.

StartFast (visit StartFast.net) was built using the world-leading Techstars model for venture accelerators (visit TechStars.com). This model is entrepreneur-led and populated with a highly curated mentor roster that emphasizes the give first philosophy, helping minimize takers who seek transactional benefit and instead focusing on building a successful program that values mentors helping first-time entrepreneurs.

You can find more information about how to build your own venture accelerator on this best practices model by using Techstars' open-source playbook, made available through the Global Accelerator Network (visit GAN.co).

There's nothing that scares away a highly influential person more than abstractly asking for their support with a big request that the foundation has not yet been built for. A more reasonable ask might be for them to share their story of success with a local audience or to provide their expertise to solve a specific problem you're dealing with.

Here's an example, so you can see how these various pieces fit together. At UVC's 2018 annual Upstate Unleashed, our keynote speaker was Marc Randolph, the founding CEO of Netflix. This man is as opportunity-rich as you could possibly imagine. How did we get him to go cross-country to speak in Upstate New York?

My process began with research to identify high-profile alumni from Upstate colleges, and that effort discovered Marc Randolph was a graduate of Hamilton College in Clinton, New York.

I immediately put him on our target list and set out to find a way to connect with him by being referred by a trusted source who knew us both.

Since there were about a half dozen possible intermediaries I identified through LinkedIn, my next step was to contact each one to see who knew Marc well enough to queue up an intro for me.

One of those outreach contacts was to First Round Capital partner Bill Trenchard, mentioned earlier in the chapter. Bill confirmed his strength of relationship was there with Marc, and he put my request for contact in motion.

After several email exchanges with Marc over a few months, we had a get-acquainted phone call, then a personal meeting while I was in the Bay Area. There I pitched him on giving the keynote for the Upstate Unleashed conference, and he agreed. I succeeded because I made gradual progress with him by keeping him informed of our activities, and I didn't harangue him too early. Even with the original introduction from Bill Trenchard, if my first interaction was an email request asking him to keynote the UVC conference he'd never heard of, there is little chance he would have been interested.

For some highly influential people, what we consider to be a small ask might be too much until we've proven the value of what we're doing. So we've found it best to start with the smallest ask the HIP is likely to say yes to. Asking for one specific piece of advice or one specific introduction can be a starting point. And throughout the dialogue, gather information about what the interests of the other party might be. The combination of small asks and greater understanding of the HIP's interests help us deepen the relationship, demonstrate the importance of our mission, and show we are committed to take action to collaborate.

The smallest ask of all is to stay in communication. With UVC, we keep people informed through our newsletter and Twitter, Facebook, and LinkedIn networks. Even if highly influential people don't read every communication we send out, just by their seeing there is a steady stream of new content, we ensure the name of our organization and our mission stay top of mind, and prove that we are not a flash in the pan dependent on the good intentions of a single person.

HIGHLY INFLUENTIAL PEOPLE ARE PASSIONATE ABOUT HELPING

After a decade doing this work, I can say for certain that the right highly influential people can be passionate about helping young entrepreneurs thrive. I've consistently been amazed and impressed with the kindness and generosity of the busy and powerful people who have supported us.

As you might expect, not all of these outreaches turn into productive relationships, even with people who seem to be a fit based on their community interests and intentions. When we sit down to talk about our mission, what we typically find is that they want to help—but just aren't sure how to do it in a way that makes sense for them.

They understand *intellectually* that our community doesn't have enough opportunities for young entrepreneurs to succeed in newer industries. Understanding that is easy. What is elusive for them is seeing the path of how they personally can make an impact, since local HIPs without experience in the newer industries say things like "I don't know anything about technology so I don't see how I can have high impact." Our job is to bridge that gap to what is possible and relevant for them.

This is best done in either one-on-one dialogues or in small group settings involving a credible HIP to share relevant insights.

One of the best such interactions I've had the chance to take part in was a fireside chat featuring Marc Randolph the morning after his keynote address at our Upstate Unleashed conference. We gathered about twenty-five entrepreneurs and HIPs for an intimate breakfast event where I was able to interview Marc before the group as he shared insights on his post-Netflix effort in helping a Santa Cruz–based entrepreneur, who in turn ended up revitalizing the downtown Santa Cruz area and launching a successful startup ecosystem there.

Marc shared the background of how he was assisted by a forward-looking local real estate developer who made a commitment for office space outside the norms for the area that proved to be crucial for helping both Marc's new company and the overall downtown of Santa Cruz.

Our assembled audience included real estate developers, college and community leaders, entrepreneurs, and potential startup investors—all of whom came away with a heightened sense of purpose and, most importantly, the understanding that even without a background in tech there were ways they could deploy their network and resources to help take part in a private-sector-led effort to grow a startup community that would create more good jobs.

Without understanding the context of the situation, too often these same people wouldn't realize the ripple effects that their support can have on the total jobs in a community. They wouldn't see how their contributions can be part of something that could make a real difference, and there's nothing that successful entrepreneurs hate more than taking action that doesn't lead to an impact. We have to show them that impact if we want the HIPs to get engaged.

Many successful people overlook how their wisdom is taken for granted. As the years have gone by in their careers, some may have begun to think of their wisdom as common sense and forget what it was like to be a new entrepreneur starting off. They may overlook how valuable their ideas and support would be for young startups.

It's our job to remind them of these things. We don't need to convince them or tell them what to believe. We just need to show them that their actions *do* make an impact on the community and give them a clear, actionable way to help.

When we do these things, highly influential people surprise us with their generosity and commitment.

SUMMARY

- Early adopters in the form of highly influential people will give your movement quick credibility and supercharge your efforts.
- Look for HIPs who are successful, give first, and have credibility in the local community.
- Don't limit yourself to your local area. Also explore those who can help from neighboring communities, or even those with useful skillsets in other geographies, including those that have moved away but still have affinity for the community.
- When engaging HIPs, always make a specific ask.
- Don't make too big of an ask right away. HIPs are busy, and you don't want to burden them.
- HIPs generally want to help. Make it clear why their time will be truly impactful to your community, and they may surprise you with their generosity.
- Building a private network of HIPs that you bring together for furthering ecosystem goals is a powerful way to spread connectivity and impact.

CHAPTER 7

ENGAGING EARLY-STAGE PRIVATE CAPITAL

HOW TO START GROWING POOLS OF PRIVATE CAPITAL FOR STARTUPS

No one has ever become poor by giving.

—ANNE FRANK

Investors with private capital are often thought of at the center of startup ecosystems, but not always for the right reasons. Of course, capital matters for startups, but in its most effective form, private capital is a critical path to spur engagement of highly influential people in your community's startup scene. Not just by getting them to write investment checks, but by getting a portion of their time, expertise, and relationships pointed in the direction of next-generation entrepreneurs.

With engagement of HIPs, capital and talent can start to flow from the sidelines and into the game of helping build the local startup ecosystem that entrepreneurs will want to take advantage of.

WHY DOES PRIVATE CAPITAL MATTER?

Imagine walking into a startup meetup and asking the first founder you meet why private capital matters for startups. If they're like most founders, they will look at you with a blank stare of silent confusion. Asking a founder why capital matters is like asking a fish why water matters—it's such a ubiquitous part of their ecosystem that they can't even imagine a world without it.

There are critics of startup culture who point to the assumptions around the requirement to raise outside capital as a problem with the startup model.

In some cases, this criticism is fair. There are certainly companies that raise money and use it wastefully, and at the other end of the spectrum are bootstrapped startups that forge a growth path without having to depend on outside investors. However, for most startups, the journey of building an innovation-based company will be reliant on outside capital.

Capital is a necessary ingredient to create innovation economy companies. These companies are, by their nature, doing something new and different that the market has not yet broadly adopted. In most cases, they aren't copying an existing model with an existing market—they're creating their own markets.

And while it can be helpful to be first to market with a new product or service, ultimately it is successful execution in building a company that matters more than the idea of the innovation itself. Google's late start and eventual triumph in search over the well-established Yahoo and Microsoft search engines would be just one well-known example.

Even more relevant for our themes here would be the demise of Lawrence, Kansas–based ProFusion, a company first to market with a cutting-edge search engine product in 1994 that was lauded by *PC Magazine* in 1997 as "Editor's Choice" for the world's best meta search engine. With well over a million users a month—such eye-popping traffic for those early days of the World Wide Web—the young Google team even approached ProFusion founders to inquire how ProFusion might help drive traffic to Google!

But about that same time, Yahoo was already much further ahead in its development as a company, having raised more than $35 million in capital that it began deploying to buy up other startups with products that could fit into the Yahoo suite.

Notwithstanding what was a superior technical product at the time, ProFusion ended up getting crushed by Yahoo well before the Google juggernaut found its footing.

As the story is profiled in Victor Hwang and Greg Horowitt's insightful book *Rainforest: Secrets to Growing the Next Silicon Valley*, the comparison of how Lawrence, Kansas's lack of a supportive community with what Yahoo was surrounded by in Silicon Valley goes to the heart of how Yahoo, even with an inferior product, took full advantage of that supportive community to raise boatloads of funding, build the team, and successfully penetrate the dot-com era's hyper-growth search engine market.

WHY DO INNOVATION COMPANIES CONSUME SO MUCH STARTUP CAPITAL?

It's not hard to see that creating anything unproven in the market is more expensive than copying an existing business model and proven set of processes that customers are familiar with. Whether the startup is creating a product, service, or technology, there is a lot of problem-solving and customer discovery required to iterate a solution that can scale up to large volume adoption beyond a local marketplace.

Sometimes with a narrow, technology-based innovation that is timed to ride a host of marketplace drivers and a viral path to rapid adoption (e.g., WhatsApp, Instagram, etc.), it is possible for this growth to scale up incredibly quickly. But these are the exceptions, not the norm, as most businesses will go through a series of iterations to tune both the product/service and the path to growing new customers.

Even with an impressive new offering based on innovation, the challenge of educating customers to become early adopters is a big hurdle when you are asking them to stop doing something they are already familiar with. People are naturally resistant to change, so there's a burden of proof on the startup to show why the new solution is better in a way that the customer never heard of or thought about before.

Startups also have to ensure that customers understand that the risk they're taking by trying an innovative product won't backfire. For example, if you opened a hotel, people would instantly understand what you do. But as Airbnb found, even with their Silicon Valley start and backing of legendary startup investor Paul Graham through his Y Combinator (visit YCombinator.com), it proved to be a lengthy process of discovering the right mix of education paths and risk-mitigation mechanisms to drive adoption for allowing strangers to sleep in one's own home.

To make matters even more difficult, many of the innovation economy offerings can be in sectors rife with competitors due to low barriers to entry. Into the late nineties, if you wanted to create a product or service for the internet, you were burdened with an enormous amount of cash-burning overhead. Creating a digital technology platform required you to essentially own and operate your own proprietary data center. It just wasn't feasible for most new companies unless they had already raised millions in startup capital.

Now, by taking advantage of cloud-based services such as Amazon Web Services or Microsoft Azure, plus prebuilt shopping carts and other online transaction tools, you can build a professional website and start selling your product or service in a single afternoon. Leveraging resources like these makes it possible for anyone with an idea to create a business cheaply and quickly—thereby creating a lot of room for competitive entry at the low end.

Scaling up from that low-end offering that anyone can construct requires a combination of something truly innovative and a disciplined execution to cut through the crowded landscape with the continual iteration needed to refine the offering as well as raise customer awareness and adoption.

Product and market development in newer industries requires expensive talent—people who already have plenty of other opportunities and sufficient demand for their specialized skills that they are not going to be hired on the cheap. A whole team of innovative talent is needed—and it's not realistic to assume that the innovation of a single founder will be enough to cover all the functions encompassed in building a true company that scales up to meaningful levels in headcount and revenue.

So the vast majority of innovation companies are hard-pressed to launch and grow revenues fast enough to cover product- and market-development expenses before being overtaken by a new innovation developed in someone's garage or accelerator program, which then raises capital to grow the market opportunity sooner than the bootstrapped entrepreneur can do it on their own.

With these factors in mind, you can imagine how difficult it can be for an innovation company to succeed without external capital. It simply won't have sufficient revenue growth soon enough to power through the long product- and customer-development cycle.

Raising outside debt funding is not a realistic option for startups. Banks are especially notorious for lending money only to those who have already proven their ability to repay. They like to give money to companies that have a long track record of stability and already have assets that can be used as collateral.

Startups, on the other hand, generally have few assets, little or no revenue, and are unlikely to qualify for traditional bank financing or Small Business Administration loans.

Almost all aspiring startup entrepreneurs exploring a new idea are quickly faced with the question: *how am I going to get the capital necessary to take my idea from concept through the product- and market-development phase to actually generate enough revenue to cover expenses?*

With banks and other traditional capital options out of the question, unless they're able to tap the assets of some wealthy friends or relatives, they're left with only one path: private equity capital.

THE SHORTAGE OF SEED CAPITAL INVESTORS IN TALENT-EXPORTING CITIES

In most of our Talent Exporting Cities, people with personal capital are often on the sidelines. Sidelined capital means locked up potential for both startup entrepreneurs and the community. Even if there are emerging companies in our community worth investing in, the individual people with capital don't know about or have interest in them, so the potential opportunities remain unexplored.

In communities where startup investing isn't common, people with financial capacity often don't even consider it as a possibility. This shortage of active private capital investors in Talent Exporting Cities comes from three dynamics.

First, people in Talent Exporting Cities with financial capacity likely have a shortage of local role models to look at as successful investments. They probably don't know anyone in the community already doing seed investing, don't know how to get started, and don't trust their judgment in evaluating potential investments in sectors they are not already personally familiar with. Because they don't see others succeeding, they stay on the sidelines.

Second, and even worse, sidelined money begets sidelined money. Many potential investors get into the game when they see their friends, colleagues, or role models succeeding in their investments. Without an initial spark of private capital investors succeeding and sharing their success with others, it seems like an impossible climb to build momentum toward getting a herd moving in the same direction.

Last, there are also subtle but powerful generational dynamics that keep private capital investors from financing innovative companies. It all comes down to a fundamental fact of innovation and wealth acquisition: the people with capital are often from the generation preceding the entrepreneurs needing startup capital.

Right now, private capital investors are most likely baby boomers investing in millennials who have companies utilizing advanced technology, new innovations, and new business models. Investors from the older generation are less likely to be familiar with the forefront of today's innovation. Instead of exploring how to embrace these opportunities, we hear the boomers say things like "I don't understand your company. I haven't seen it work for anyone else. Why should I invest?" As a result, the boomers keep their money pocketed and everyone loses.

Another reason private capital investors sit on the sidelines is because they talk to their accountants, investment managers, and other advisors, each of whom is being paid to guide their client toward minimizing risks. So it is no wonder that when the client comes in with bubbling enthusiasm to make a startup investment, their advisors are quick to respond with remarks like "Investing in a privately held company in a new, untested industry is the stupidest thing you could do with your wealth. You'll have no control, your investment won't be liquid anytime soon (if ever), and once you make that investment you cannot reverse it. If you want to make that choice, you might as well write off every dollar you invest."

All this is made worse by the high standards to qualify by federal standards as an accredited investor, which is necessary in order to be eligible to make investments in private companies.

In general terms, to meet the federal accredited investor standard, you have to have net assets (not including your personal residence) of greater than $1 million for two or more consecutive years and have an annual income of $200,000 or more filing as a single taxpayer ($300,000 or more if filing a joint return). If you don't meet those qualifications, with the exception of limited amounts that can be contributed through crowdfunding, you're not allowed to invest in private companies.

Private capital investors aren't only discouraged to invest in innovation economy companies by their financial advisors, their accountants, and the government; unless they are hanging out with others who've successfully invested in startups, they are likely to be discouraged by their peers. Everyone can think of the risky elements, but without visible role models and objective information on how to mitigate risk (much less understand how the community benefits), it is far too easy to see the negatives outweighing the upside.

ABUNDANCE OF SEED CAPITAL IN MAGNET CITIES

While these same financial risk elements exist in Magnet Cities where an innovation economy flourishes, there is a completely different paradigm with regard to the accessibility of early-stage capital for startups.

The volume of exits (liquidity events where the sale, recapitalization, or IPO of a company returned money to investors) go well beyond the multibillion-dollar windfalls that make national headlines. Companies exiting for $5 million to $20 million after only three to five years in business can provide impressive returns, depending on how capital-efficient the startup was in that time period.

And with hundreds or more exits per year in a Magnet City, so grows the pool of money from both exiting investors and team members of the company achieving the exit.

Even in a large metro area like New York City, folks plugged into the innovation economy have efficient communication channels, so exit news spreads via the winners and community members as well as some who lament on their having missed the opportunity to invest.

In fact, there are so many people who have succeeded by investing in Magnet City innovation economy companies that angel investing in new ideas is something that wealthy individuals are irrationally *more* likely to do.

And the boomer investors are supplemented by a new class of wealthy exited entrepreneurs or investors who are disproportionately young compared to those who have self-made wealth in Talent Exporting Cities. Plus the Magnet City financial advisors all have other clients who have made millions in startup investing.

Ongoing chatter about exits is the talk of the town, planting seeds for aspiring entrepreneurs to launch a company and drawing the next accredited investor off the sidelines and into the game. It's just the cool scene everyone wants to be part of.

All of this combines to create a surplus of capital and high valuations of companies looking for those investment dollars in Magnet Cities. It's the virtuous cycle where success begets more success as the Magnet Cities attract the next generation of entrepreneurs from well outside their boundaries who are fleeing their capital-starved Talent Exporting Cities for the voluminous money wells they hear exist elsewhere.

GETTING INVESTORS OFF THE SIDELINES AND INTO THE GAME

Funding challenges like these in Talent Exporting Cities are based on people's ingrained beliefs. They aren't going to be solved with some advertising about how low-cost the Talent Exporting Cities are or how attractive the quality of life there is, or be changed with some silver-bullet public policy.

Perspectives have to change from the ground up, which means slowly, one relationship at a time, probably over an extended time period.

One such belief is seeing startup investing as a mix of both community support and investment. Similar to many philanthropic efforts, angel investing is a great way to give back, build up the community, create more jobs, and provide value to others. While angel investing has the potential to create a great return on investment, older potential investors can come to see their investments as their responsibility to give back to the next generation in their community, rather than pure return-on-investment calculations.

Beyond changing people's beliefs, there are some things we can do to help create the environment that gets potential investors off of the sidelines and into the game. As a result, we can begin to build the data points necessary to change these beliefs.

The typical response to this problem is to start an angel network. High-net-worth individuals get together for a supper club where entrepreneurs pitch ideas. If any of the members of the angel network are interested, they invest individually.

This model can sometimes produce an exit, but it's difficult and suboptimal for individual investors. Attendees are making decisions on their own; they're making bets that have long-term implications and perhaps not realizing that they are likely to be called again for more capital as the company grows. As a result, the novice angel investor ends up with a deep position in just one or two companies, thereby creating much more downside risk if just one investment flames out.

Most investors know that the best way to successfully invest in startups is by investing in a portfolio of companies. Yet, for the individual angel investor who has less than $1 million or so to invest, this isn't always possible.

For this reason, instead of an angel network, what we've found to work best for newbie startup investors is to instead concentrate on launching a member-managed seed capital fund. We might end up working with some of the same people from an angel network, who can now be investing similar dollar levels as before, but by using a fund arrangement, they get the benefit of portfolio diversification and a team-supported approach.

Here are some quick takes on the process to establish a seed fund:

- Get some best-practices input and then begin developing a fund pitch deck that establishes investment goals, structure, and a high-level view of the target companies to be invested in.

- Socialize the proposed fund structure beginning with some investors who might have been part of an existing angel network, but cast a wider net to also find others, as the fund has more to offer than any informal network.
- Define the fund's governance process on how the group of investors makes decisions to invest the fund's money, so any investment is made on behalf of all of the investors.
- Set expectations for investors on how they'll participate in doing the work involved in finding qualified deal flow, evaluating prospective investments, and most importantly, helping the fund's portfolio firms after the investment check has been written.

You can immediately see the ways in which this might solve the common challenges raised by those shouting, "Startup investing is too risky!" By pooling resources, investors can invest in a far more diverse portfolio. With a larger group of investors having "skin in the game," entrepreneurs will now have a broader base of support to call upon, rather than just a couple individual investors who might have invested as the result of an angel network introduction. In other words, creating a seed fund brings together the community to support the newly funded entrepreneur.

Since the fund is operated by volunteers, this is referred to as a *member-managed* seed capital fund. Rather than creating competition between private capital investors, the members actually get their money off the sidelines and work together in accordance with the policies and processes laid out in the fund's governance structure.

But making a seed fund work in your community is not as simple as convincing someone to write a check. There has to be a shared sense of ownership and a mutual desire to participate in doing the work involved in making a fund successful.

For example, with Upstate Venture Connect, we didn't see our role as being leaders of a fund, but rather as helping catalyze groups coming together by first identifying people in a community who were receptive to participating, then concentrating on finding and equipping one or more leaders who had the interest and personal qualities needed to engage others.

A typical angel seed fund would launch with a group of about forty to fifty individuals who commit to the fund's minimum for entry, typically ranging from $25,000 to $50,000 per investor.

Likewise, in the nascent innovation economy communities without much pitching going on, the entrepreneurs themselves need to be coached on how to present their companies to investors. For the most part, first-time entrepreneurs won't know how to present at a formal group meeting of investors. So you need to have a certain structure in place to coach entrepreneurs to pitch. Creating that structure requires significant time investments from your members.

Because a seed fund is a legal entity, you also need to create the necessary legal documents, which will serve as an operating agreement. Your operating agreement will provide governance for how group decisions are reached to make investments, what kinds of companies you're targeting, how investment gains will be distributed, responsibility for tax administration, and other issues to be compliant with security laws and transparent to the fund's limited partners.

Over the course of helping build six member-managed seed funds across Upstate New York, we've found something surprising: people with the thickest wallets almost never come aboard as investors. For super-wealthy individuals, a $50,000 investment appears too small to warrant their attention, and it doesn't help that the more money they have, the less involved they are in managing it beyond discussions with their own financial advisor.

It also seems like the more zeroes in someone's net worth, the more exclusive the crowd they want to hang out with. With these barriers and the need for seed fund members to roll up their sleeves to take an active role in sharing the work needed to make a seed fund successful, the uber-wealthy rarely come aboard as seed fund investors.

The exception would be individuals who are self-made entrepreneurs, particularly those in the newer industries (see profile of Jordan Levy in chapter 6), who also raised money from angel investors in the early stages of their own business journey that ultimately led to huge liquidity events. We don't see enough of those in Talent Exporting Cities, but when we do, they are certainly worth reaching out to, as they can bring more than just capital into the seed fund, even if they are not consistently showing up at the fund's monthly meeting.

Our estimate is that the majority of the members in our seed funds have a net worth in the range of $2 million to $20 million in overall assets, with much of that illiquid.

These are typically people who have enough assets to be comfortable in taking some financial risk, are mature in their business judgment, and have true passion for helping others by pledging not just a slice of their financial assets, but more importantly, their time, talents, and relationships to help first-time entrepreneurs in the community.

SOCIAL PROOF HELPS MOVE DOUBTERS TO BELIEVERS

In almost any situation where you're trying to buck the tide of accepted practices, getting public support from a credible—ideally a celebrity-level—person can be a big boost to nudge doubters toward opening their minds to something new.

Steve Case provides such a boost for Talent Exporting Cities with his high-profile Rise of the Rest tour (visit RiseOfTheRest.com). Starting in 2014, Steve and members of his Revolution team have taken multi-stop bus tours visiting more than forty mid-sized cities across America's heartland. His personal brand as co-founder and CEO of America Online and publicly visible support for entrepreneurship in media and policy circles help spark local interest in the very idea of startups having impact on the local community. These well-orchestrated pitch competitions bring startup entrepreneurs, local business and community leaders, and potential investors into the same room, as a mashup many of these communities never experienced before.

Good advance work and coordination with leaders out of the local startup community help draw a crowd for the drama of a competition awarding $100,000 in prize money per company winners, as well as the opportunity for visibility in Case's Rise of the Rest Seed and Revolution Venture funds for larger rounds of institutional financing as the best startups get traction.

The Rise of the Rest Seed Fund adds an additional layer of social proof with a roster of fund investors stacked with celebrity entrepreneurs like Jeff Bezos, Howard Schultz, Tory Burch, and Sara Blakely, to name just a few.

As we saw with the Rise of the Rest stop in Buffalo, the cumulative effect of Case's event opened up more awareness of startups, which was then followed with an uptick in new people joining the ranks of local angel seed funds.

While few people could match Steve Case's brand and resource commitment for a national tour like this, we know there are many celebrity-level entrepreneurs who have roots and affinity for their hometown Talent Exporting City. Local leaders can help cultivate that affinity with an engagement goal of going beyond a single appearance to an ongoing program where that entrepreneur's involvement can have a meaningful long-term impact on the community—perhaps beginning as an anchor investor to start your area's first seed capital fund.

SETTING UP A SEED CAPITAL FUND

Nasir Ali, my co-founder at Upstate Venture Connect, launched the Seed Capital Fund of Central New York in 2007. A newcomer to Syracuse, Nasir was asked by the Syracuse Chamber of Commerce to help increase the availability of early-stage investment capital in the region. After concluding that there might be interesting research-commercialization opportunities at the numerous colleges and universities around Syracuse, Nasir began to build relationships with tech-transfer representatives at institutions like Cornell and Syracuse University.

At the same time, he began to look at different models for angel investing and also joined the Angel Capital Association (visit AngelCapitalAssociation.org). Dissatisfied with the dinner-and-network model, where most people came to watch the pitches but few ever reached into their wallets, Nasir searched for a model that would lead to maximum angel participation (and hence the lowest amount at risk per investor). His search led him to David Ahlers, a retired Cornell professor who had started an Ithaca-based angel fund called Cayuga Venture Fund to invest in promising entrepreneurs from the local area. CVF's initial success had led to the fund evolving into a more traditional venture capital fund, with many of its original investors and funded entrepreneurs as limited partners.

With Dave as the guru willing to share his knowledge and experience, and the university research-commercialization investment strategy, Nasir reached out to a core group of four highly respected Syracuse-area business leaders, among them a retired technology executive, a real estate developer, a construction equipment dealer, and a partner at a business law firm. These four individuals assessed the opportunity, realized that Dave would be an invaluable guide, and above all, felt they could trust Nasir as an experienced fund leader who was smart, transparent, and possessed a high level of integrity. Once the core team was in agreement, it was a simple step to have them communicate their intent to create the Seed Capital Fund to others in their network and, within three months, thirty-seven of their peers agreed to write their own first checks of $37,500 each.

With the funds sitting in the bank, all the investors now had an incentive to put the money to work. Over the next three years, they met nearly every month to hear entrepreneurs pitch for funding; volunteered to perform in-depth technology, market, and founder reviews; and then voted on whether or not the fund should invest. Two more funds were created over the next three years to continue funding the portfolio companies.

As the fund investments have matured, so has the sophistication and risk profile of the participating investors. Once SCF funds were fully invested, about half of the investors stayed together to participate in a new seed-stage accelerator focused on early-stage internet businesses. A few decided to form their own partnerships and continue investing with their friends, and at least one investor decided to make the leap to becoming a limited partner in an institutional venture capital (VC) fund. While it is difficult to track the overall scale of investment created by these investors who were mostly interested in recharging the local economy, one small measure of the multiplier effect is visible from the SCF statistics. Namely, fund members contributed roughly $5.5 million to the seven SCF portfolio companies and the companies leveraged SCF's original investment to raise more than $120 million in additional funding!

Being pooled with others in a fund allows individual investors to mitigate a portion of their downside risk and increase the odds of capturing upside by spreading bets across a larger group of companies than would have been possible to do on their own with the same number of dollars to invest.

In addition to seeing the value of their investment grow, the regular meetings and engagement of group members to work together in attracting and evaluating deals, making investment decisions and mentoring early-stage entrepreneurs brought them into regular contact with other like-minded professionals who valued the chance to put their business skills to work in collaborating on something that was new and forward-looking. After SCF was fully invested, this group became the core investors forming a new type of startup investment opportunity, also led by Nasir, as we formed the StartFast Venture Accelerator, described in more detail later in this chapter.

LAUNCHING A SEED FUND REQUIRES COMMITTED LEADERSHIP

Learning from Nasir's experience in SCF, as we advanced on the mission of opening up other seed capital funds in the larger metro areas around Upstate, we knew the most critical step to getting a fund off the launchpad was finding the right leader who had the combination of skills, reputation, and relationships in the community, and passion to get it done—even though they had many other opportunities where they could place their time and resources.

We could share the playbook on how to do it, tap the UVC network and communication channels to spread the word to bring others into the fold, and even help with the initial pitches to targeted investors so we could share our experiences on why this model works.

But none of that would matter unless we could first find the right leader who was ready to personally guide the effort of engaging others in the community. The preferred leadership profile would be a recently exited entrepreneur, ideally with experience in having raised money from outside investors. But in Talent Exporting Cities like we have Upstate, there aren't yet enough of those around to tap.

Next best would be a current entrepreneur who is visible and active in the community. They might be running a stable business with a supporting management team and may be thinking about the impact they want to have on the community.

When we heard rumblings of some people in the Hudson Valley looking to start a seed fund, our search led us to Johnny LeHane, an entrepreneur in the Hudson Valley referred to us by a member of our UNY50 Leadership Network. Johnny was already busily engaged in running his business, yet his awareness of the challenges entrepreneurs faced in his capital-starved local landscape piqued his interest.

At the same time that Nasir and I were mentoring Johnny on steps involved to launch a seed fund, Tony DiMarco, director of strategic initiatives at nearby Marist College, was in discussion with Dick Frederick, another member of our UNY50 network, whom we had helped to start the Eastern New York Angels seed fund, located just one hour north of the Hudson Valley.

Because of our network connections, we were able to bring Johnny and Tony together to become key members of the founding leadership team. They went out and started finding other supporters to launch what became the Hudson Valley Startup Fund.

Neither Johnny nor Tony had startup investing experience, but they made up for that with their passion for both the community and helping entrepreneurs. Their relationships led to them bringing on three other managing members: Paul Hakim (finance and business development background), Chad Gomes (consumer products entrepreneur and strategy development guru), and Noa Simons (who had recently relocated to the area after working for a US venture capital firm in China).

The Hudson Valley Startup Fund raised and deployed $1.5 million in its initial fund, investing in six early-stage companies, all of whom remain active and growing. At the time of this book's publication, the group is closing on its second fund, with the vast majority of Fund I members increasing their stake by going into the new fund.

Leaders who put time into the work of launching an initial fund in a Talent Exporting City often find alignment between the fund effort and other interests. Even in smaller communities where they think they know everyone, the leaders invariably meet new and interesting professionals or advance their relationships with highly influential people who were previously only casual acquaintances.

As the fund grows, their reputations as leaders in the community also become more visible. This helps in other avenues, including aspects of their non-fund professional activities.

Beyond the seed fund model, two other options can increase early-stage private capital investment in Talent Exporting Cities: accelerator programs and professional venture capital.

ACCELERATOR PROGRAMS

A venture accelerator program brings a group of startups together in a cohort—usually at a very early stage—and accelerates their progress in a defined time period by providing them with structured development, exposure to best practices, and lots of hands-on guidance from program managers and experienced entrepreneurs who volunteer as mentors for the program.

Accelerators can leverage a proven curriculum and structure, emphasizing experimenting with customer discovery and lots of opportunity to play off the insights learned by other teams in the cohort. Each startup begins at about the same point of company development and is on a path to become investor-ready by the conclusion of the program twelve weeks later.

Let there be no doubt: investing in accelerator-level companies is the riskiest form of startup investing because these are truly garage-level opportunities that are far from being proven in their business model, product development, or go-to-market strategy to cost-effectively find new customers.

So the investment thesis is entirely portfolio-driven. We expect many startups will actually suffer infant mortality by failing fast. By the time the twelve-week program is up, our program managers, investors, and mentors have all had intimate contact with teams in the cohort. Even if one has not yet arrived at a stage of being investor-ready, we know if they have shown the coachability, adaptability, and resilience needed to power through the next stages of building a company.

That knowledge then helped us pick the one to three teams out of the cohort showing greatest promise for us to invest in leading a follow-on round at the conclusion of the program.

All of this sounds like a winning solution, but most accelerator programs fail. The reason has a lot to do with high expenses of running an in residence program as well as the long time it takes to get a garage-level startup to advance to a liquidity event; exits can take five to eight years from the time of accelerator program graduation. And since individual private investors want to see evidence of those returns, keeping them patient and engaged while the portfolio matures is extremely difficult in Talent Exporting Cities not brimming with news of exits.

Even with our sticking to the best-practice model pioneered by Techstars, it took five years of operating StartFast until our first major exit occurred. Over the course of that time period we had thirty-four companies complete the program, half of which are still active today.

But with the exit of just one company in our sixth year, that liquidity event returned every dollar invested in StartFast over our first five years!

With a large exit to our credit, it's a bit easier now for us to engage new investors, but none of that would have been possible had our original investors backed away from supporting us after the first couple years. Had we not been able to raise capital in years three to five, StartFast would have cratered before getting to the payday that made the difference.

LEVERAGING ACCELERATOR PROGRAM BEST PRACTICES

An accelerator program requires more resources and structure than a seed fund, but can be a good way to find early-stage companies and help them grow into job-generating engines. StartFast receive applications or touches from upwards of 250 companies each year, all of whom are screened for us to select the final companies accepted into the program. One of the ways in which we innovated was to recognize that we did not have the location or brand of a large city or big well funded accelerators like Techstars, 500 Startups or YCombinator. Rather than competing to drive inbound interest, we adopted a sophisticated strategy for identifying, qualifying and directly reaching out to promising companies that met StartFast investment criteria. For the past five years, we consistently reviewed more than 1,000 pre-seed startups.

We built the program by taking full advantage of resources made available to us by the Global Accelerator Network (visit GAN.co), a nonprofit organization that was pioneered by Techstars, the most successful accelerator program as evidenced by its truly global expansion, now spun off into what is today an independent startup accelerator network.

Startups that join accelerators are prototype-level companies that often have very little (if any) revenue. These companies are risky because their models aren't proven and they are often led by first time founders. In exchange for equity, they receive much-needed cash, and accelerator owners get the chance for early entry at low valuations, plus first-looks to get in on the next stage of investment before professional investors come in. Riding alongside the founders from an early stage of company development breeds an appreciation for the journey and special satisfaction when the startup blooms to become a larger and established company.

As described in chapter 6, part of our motivation to launch StartFast was to serve as an additional mechanism to engage Highly Influential People as high-quality mentors and resources, including those from outside our region.

Make no mistake: identifying the right mentors who are qualified and participating to give first is the backbone behind starting an accelerator. Finding companies and creating a curriculum are easy relative to the task of fielding an accelerator program leadership team who are then rounded out with capable volunteer mentors.

However, this is where the value lies in building the ecosystem. More than anything, accelerator programs and seed funds with active investors can be a way to bridge the gap between the private capital and expertise now sitting on the sidelines, getting them engaged in supporting the startups in our community.

CAN VIRTUAL ACCELERATORS WORK?

We sometimes see virtual accelerators promoted as a path to help startups. Not having the overhead of a place-based program reduces the expenses, and with today's widespread acceptance of video teleconferencing for meetings, some believe this is a cost-effective way to educate entrepreneurs.

Having been through multiple cohorts with StartFast, we've seen the value of a place-based accelerator. The intimacy of interactions between teams in an in-residence accelerator cohort, as well as with program investors and mentors, can be higher quality in-person as opposed to virtual.

However, as the COVID-19 pandemic swept across the country in 2020, an in-residence program was not an option for StartFast and we re-evaluated the accelerator landscape along with our long-term program goals. We noted that even though the GAN.co website shows over 100 accelerators, very few in smaller markets like ours are relying purely on private investor capital. Most accelerators now receive support from some combination of public money and corporate sponsorship as an important base level of funding for program management and overhead. We also noted that very few accelerators are able to sustain themselves for the long term in smaller cities, unless they were already a Magnet City.

Knowing that the best startup candidates would not be able to relocate to Upstate New York for the program, we shifted to an entirely virtual offering that continued to take advantage of our actively engaged investors and mentors. The four companies we selected in our 2020 cohort ended up being among the highest quality in our 9 years of running the program. Furthermore, they included two startups from Rochester, NY that would have found it difficult to make the move to Syracuse (a mere 90 miles away).

Leveraging our strong base of active contributors is enabling StartFast to evolve into a professionally managed seed to Series A fund powered by an actively engaged network of entrepreneur mentors and investors. We'll continue the community building aspects of StartFast and, with a larger base of capital, our plan is to have even greater capability to help more companies across our Upstate region.

We have a saying in the early-stage investing world: *Writing the first check is easy. The hard part is helping the company become successful after you've made that investment.* Seed funds and accelerator programs with active investors and mentors can provide a track to run on that engages community assets to work on developing promising early-stage companies in a high-impact way.

GNARLY PROBLEMS IN SELECTING COMPANIES

Throughout UVC's journey in helping others start seed capital funds and accelerator programs, we consistently see one gut-wrenching issue that has to be thought through at the very inception of building support from investors: should the invested companies be limited to local entrepreneurs or should the emphasis be on finding and selecting companies that are most likely to drive returns for investors?

If you reflect on many of the themes we've already touched on in the book, it is easy to see there can be greater passion from local investors who want to limit their capital to local firms that are most likely to remain in the area. After all, that's very much the intent behind working toward the community outcomes we've been talking about.

The flip side is that if the fund or accelerator doesn't proceed on a success path to actually make money for private capital investors, the community base fund will inevitably dry up, as these are supposed to be investments, not charitable contributions.

Over the decade that Nasir and I have worked through this with each of the funds and accelerator programs we've touched, we have consistently advocated for having the fund or accelerator portfolio targets not be limited to local entrepreneurs and companies, and instead be aimed squarely toward companies having the highest probability of generating a return for investors.

We do all we can to encourage fund documents and marketing to take a broader view of who is eligible to participate as a company in the portfolio. Of course, angels will gravitate toward the local opportunities since it is in line with the reason for them signing up. But we caution about the "picking the least weak idea" problem that inevitably occurs when a new fund puts restrictive geographic limitations on who can participate.

Our guidance is that the fund or program's governance structure has to provide for the right process in evaluating investment opportunities that balance the interest of supporting local community goals with the absolute requirement that the investment vehicle has to be profitable. These are not government programs where public funds are being deployed. Each dollar is coming out of a participant's wallet with the intent of getting a return.

Our most successful seed funds and accelerators have adopted this approach of making investor return the primary screen, noting that when a nonlocal investment is made, there are local advocates that include people who can add value to the investment and relationships that can spill across geographic lines. Even if the successful company is not headquartered in the accelerator city, our experience is that exit returns flow back into the local economy and engaged mentors and investors can create strong local business connections that result in local jobs.

Since UVC also connects the investors of the six funds, a company receiving the first round at one seed capital fund can be supported by investors from other geographies in later rounds of funding.

PROFESSIONAL VENTURE CAPITAL FIRMS

While seed funds and accelerator programs are great at helping nascent startups get off the ground, at a certain size, the innovation companies gaining market traction require more capital than these programs can provide.

The next stage of financing is with true institutional money known as venture capital. In a series A offering, the first stage of venture capital, startups are often raising a round in the range of $3 million to $5 million.

VCs are private equity investors who have a fiduciary responsibility to represent the interests of the limited partners providing the fund's capital—typically from institutional sources like pension funds, insurance companies, endowments from colleges or large nonprofits, other investment houses, and very wealthy families.

Since they're writing larger checks than angels and have a fiduciary responsibility to their limited partnerships, VC professionals go through much more extensive due diligence in screening their investment choices and taking a very hands-on approach to helping guide the management teams of companies in their portfolio, both in a governance capacity (e.g., being on the company's board of directors), as well as providing strategic guidance and helping connect the management team with needed resources appropriate for the company's stage of development.

Because series A is the riskiest slice of institutional investment pie, next to seed capital this is also the least accessible to startups in Talent Exporting Cities.

In the big Magnet Cities, series A investors are visible and accessible. In places like Upstate New York, even after a startup has advanced through seed financing and has some market traction, this is the next big funding gap where promising startups will start falling off the cliff into oblivion because they are unable to raise institutional growth capital to take advantage of the traction they've now proven in the marketplace.

Typically, new series A–level VC funds get started by exiting entrepreneurs who begin with some of their own capital, supplemented by institutional investors they know who are receptive to supporting a first-time fund. Again, this is more common in Magnet Cities, since that is where you will have plenty of exiting entrepreneurs and also a network of personal and institutional relationships receptive to the opportunity of investing in early-stage companies.

Getting a series A fund started in a Talent Exporting City has some obvious obstacles:

- There aren't many local exiting entrepreneurs with $10 million-plus of personal capital to invest.
- There is a dearth of personal and institutional investors interested in (much less experienced with) startup investing.
- No one knows if there are enough fundable startups out there for the new series A fund to be competitive in the very crowded space of series A investment.
- Even if the new series A fund invested in an area company, what happens if that funded startup then leaves for a Magnet City where it could find more talent?

While Upstate Venture Connect has concentrated on the seed capital funding gap, we helped support a novel approach taken by one of our communities that grasped the significance of the series A funding gap and then went out and did something about it.

Rob Simpson, CEO of Syracuse-based nonprofit economic development organization CenterState CEO, was the leader who put this one together. Beginning with institutional relationships Rob and the CenterState team had with Syracuse University and several local corporations, Rob got buy-in to the idea that if a small consortium of investors could cobble together an initial $5 million to $7 million in commitments, that would be enough to run a process whereby CenterState could recruit an experienced venture capital professional, who would then lead the effort to attract more capital, closer to the targeted $10 million to $15 million needed to start doing series A deals.

Rob also knew that many of the wealthiest local families were sitting on the sidelines and not involved with the seed fund or accelerator programs, yet were people with a passion for helping the next-generation entrepreneurs and local job growth who might be tapped, as they could now write larger checks and have the comfort of working through professional rather than volunteer managers. This construct was much more amenable to the kind of investment decision they could now review with their investment advisors.

All of this unfolded right in line with Rob's vision. The initial commitments were made, and CenterState then had the credibility to recruit Somak Chattopadhyay, a highly qualified venture capital professional who relocated from New York City to Upstate and began reeling in other institutional investors needed to grow the new Armory Square Ventures to reach its target fund size.

In just three years from inception, Armory made eight series A investments, some of those advancing to follow-on rounds involving syndication with larger VC firms, as the entire portfolio is moving in the right direction. One of Armory's notable investments was in ACV Auctions (a Buffalo company originally birthed in Jordan Levy's Z80 Labs, mentioned in chapter 6), which has now advanced to unicorn status as a private company that investors have valued in excess of $1 billion.

As one of Armory's limited partners, I'm more than a little impressed with the rapid progress Somak and team have made in building a quality portfolio from scratch. Other investors are ecstatic as well, and Armory has cruised in to raising its next fund, showing that an investment thesis of deploying capital into the overlooked market of Upstate New York has an appeal that is now bringing in both previously reluctant local wealthy families as well as outside money to take part.

Local community leadership led by CenterState CEO and the Armory team is a shining example of how it is possible to pull together individuals *and* organizations to participate in the next stage of financing, and do it in a way that pushes private capital off of the sidelines and into the community.

Building a thriving, innovative community will not be possible without getting private capital invested in startups. With such low barriers to entry for startups, the companies having the best shot to expand rapidly once they prove market traction will be those that have avenues to tap private equity capital.

We've found that Talent Exporting Cities, instead of wringing their hands over a lack of capital to fuel young companies, have options to change the dynamic. From catalyzing the formation of seed capital funds, accelerator programs, or even professionally managed venture capital firms, it is possible to bridge the capital gap by getting those people with financial capacity off the sidelines and into the game.

It begins with a clear vision, adoption of proven best practices, and a relentless pursuit of seeking out the right people who share the view of being in it for the long haul.

SUMMARY

- An abundance of private capital is a necessity to create a thriving Magnet City, because investment is needed to encourage the creation of new innovation economy companies.
- There's a shortage of private capital in Talent Exporting Cities because high-net-worth individuals aren't exposed to the successes and are constantly reminded by others that it's too risky.
- The typical response is to start an angel network, but this doesn't tend to produce meaningful results. The better way to get people off the sidelines and into the game is by launching a member-managed seed capital fund.
- The biggest challenge to starting a seed fund is finding the right leader.
- You can also encourage investment through accelerator programs and building a consortium of initial capital to catalyze an institutional series A fund managed by a venture capital professional.
- The goal of these programs isn't just to provide funding for startups, but also to get more experienced entrepreneurs and highly influential people into the game. These are the people who have the interest and capacity to be helping next-generation companies transform your community from talent-exporting to Magnet City.

CHAPTER 8

ENGAGING HIGHER ED

HOW TO UNLOCK HUMAN CAPITAL
SILOED INSIDE UNIVERSITIES

We build too many walls and not enough bridges.
—ISAAC NEWTON

A region's higher education institutions have the potential to be the source of the area's most valuable resource: talented young people.

However, that's not how it normally plays out in Talent Exporting Cities.

Instead of attracting, developing, and keeping talented young people in the area, colleges in most tier 2 and tier 3 markets bring in an influx of talent and then, at the end of four years, send them on their way to find opportunities elsewhere.

This is an enormous wasted opportunity. Here in Upstate New York, we have more than one hundred colleges and universities that collectively enroll a half million students. More specifically, we have one of the largest concentrations of STEM programs of any region in the country, which has led to the allocation of more than $2 billion in research and development in Upstate colleges and corporations.

We graduate between 100,000 and 125,000 students every year. But far too many of our graduates leave Upstate after they graduate. In other words, our colleges and universities are amazing at attracting talented people from all over the world, and yet we don't provide them with good enough opportunities to keep them here. Even if they grew up here, they leave for greener pastures as the new wave of students comes in. The people we're losing are our future leaders, and we casually watch them walk away after putting our time and tax dollars into nurturing them.

Not only is it a lost opportunity for local economies, but for grads who are originally from the region where the college is located, their exodus also has a devastating impact on family relationships as parents and other family members realize that for the rest of their lives they will only see the departing grad as an occasional visitor.

Such is the story across the country in Talent Exporting Cities: young talent grows up locally or comes in for an education, then leaves after graduation.

This is the crux of the Retainment Quotient analysis we performed, as discussed in chapters 1 and 2. To become a Magnet City, we have to support our communities in keeping graduating students to start and/or work at innovation economy companies locally.

It's inevitable that most students aiming for work in the newer industries will relocate after graduating college in a

Talent Exporting City. But think about leverage gained by simply slowing the attrition rate of just a portion of the top tier of talent with the strongest interest in the innovation economy opportunities—both for seeking employment and, especially, for students graduating with entrepreneurial ambition.

Here's the biggest opportunity for engaging with higher education: the greater the number of students who start getting grounded in off-campus innovation economy activity, the more likely they are to become a part of the community and see the opportunities that exist for them after graduation.

Cultivating relationships for young people who have interests in innovation economy opportunities could be argued to be a truly high-impact outcome for a college in a Talent Exporting City. Yet colleges in Talent Exporting Cities across the country neglect their students' entrepreneurial spirit. Even universities that offer entrepreneurship majors and minors—which sounds like a logical first step—often fail to help students plug into the local entrepreneurial community.

As we work with higher education institutions to improve our communities, our focus should be on serving their students in a way that fosters entrepreneurial spirit and providing them with the connections and opportunities they need to stay in our communities after they graduate.

THE ABSENCE OF EXPERIENTIAL LEARNING IN HIGHER EDUCATION

Student interest in entrepreneurship is growing. Colleges and universities have recognized this demand, but for the most part, the entrepreneurship programs we see rarely produce the targeted outcomes of students becoming adequately prepared and connected to start their own company following graduation.

Across the country, we see colleges slapping an entrepreneurship major together by doing nothing more than looping together courses in their existing curricula and adding a few new ones with entrepreneurial titles. These programs are often housed in the college's business school, not recognizing that entrepreneurship is multidisciplinary, with the innovations and student interest coming out of every other curriculum on the campus.

However, there is an even bigger picture that schools miss: entrepreneurs don't learn through lectures; they learn by doing.

The current college education model doesn't align well with teaching a subject like entrepreneurship. With the typical college format grounded in lectures, writing papers, and taking tests, there is almost no learning through hands-on experience of iterating, with market feedback at each stage of evolution, as is done in any startup. There is no learning with the essential element of feedback provided by customers driving the next set of decisions. There is no learning by doing.

Credibility in the world of academia—whether through years teaching, publications, or awards—doesn't matter to entrepreneurship students. They want to learn from real entrepreneurs with real experience in the real world. And while a small amount of lecture might be involved, the opportunity to learn through the students' own hands-on development of actual businesses is how they acquire the needed knowledge and skills through experiential learning.

We've seen similar challenges in the world of college-level computer science. Any employer who hires entry-level coders will tell you that most computer science graduates come out of college ill-equipped to do even basic work needed by companies. Why? Because in college they didn't learn practical coding relevant to today's businesses. Students sit through lectures, get tested on theoretical concepts, and perhaps dabble lightly to show low levels of proficiency on outdated software platforms no longer in use at most companies.

These educational shortcomings are the reasons why commercial coding academies have become such a success. For example, Galvanize is a twenty-four-week commercial coding course that costs $21,000. That's a lot of money for a twenty-four-week program, but by the time they finish, 87 percent of the graduates have a job offer, with an average starting salary of $70,000. Colleges have students for four years, and they don't produce anything close to those results.

Coding academies work because they focus on the student learning by doing actual projects that are similar in scope and approach to what is done inside most companies, using the same software platforms and tools used in companies today.

Coding academies are more in a coaching model instead of lecture format. Students work through a series of online tutorials on their own, getting help from the coach when they get stuck. Projects include team-based assignments, with a small group of students collaborating using a combination of different tools and approaches. The total focus is on an experiential learning process that has more parallels to how platform development works inside today's companies.

Coding academy instructors are valued on two important factors: (1) competency in their own coding skills using state-of-the-art platforms, and (2) personal qualities needed to help nontechnical people acquire these skills. Their formal educational background doesn't matter, nor whether they have any publications or institutional teaching experience in their background.

Another head-scratching example of the gap between college offerings and marketplace need is the absence of professional sales as a major. Collegiate business programs across the country routinely feature marketing as a major, but I have yet to come across programs with an actual sales major, where the focus was on developing skills using the experiential learning model needed for actual selling.

Any CEO will tell you there are twenty times or more opportunities in sales for each marketing role, and sales roles are among the hardest to find top talent for. The supply/demand imbalance is so out of whack that it is reflected in much higher compensation levels needed to attract and retain the best talent.

Students aspiring to become entrepreneurs will certainly take advantage of sales-related courses and majors as they understand how important that function is for the overall success in developing a company.

As with entrepreneurship and coding, the skillsets you would want an instructor to have to help students be successful in sales do not line up with what the traditional academic community values in terms of advanced degrees, research, publications, teaching experience at other colleges, etc.

So, whether it's process for experiential learning, degree curricula, or profile of who is best qualified to help students prepare for acquiring skills in these high-value areas, most colleges seem more intent on muddling along, with the higher priority being to remain wedded to traditional academic norms ahead of adapting to what the marketplace really needs in the rapidly changing world of innovation companies.

BARRIERS TO CONNECTING STUDENTS TO LOCAL RESOURCES

It's one thing to graduate students without coding, sales, or entrepreneurship skillsets. But the larger disservice colleges and universities are doing is not providing students with enough opportunities to build valuable business *relationships*.

Building relationships will not only benefit students while they're in school, it also prepares them for their career and lives after graduating.

We've discussed at length the importance of relationships for success in the world of entrepreneurship. For such a high-impact need, colleges do very little to provide students with the training and opportunities to develop their personal network, particularly with local resources that might be off campus. Without an emphasis on expanding their personal network of relationships, young people can go through college cocooned from the community at large who can help them. (For techniques and an understanding of why it's so important to grow your personal network, I highly recommend Pat Hedley's excellent book *Meet 100 People*.)

Whether you're an academic or a local community leader, if you're seeking to build a stronger entrepreneur-supporting ecosystem, there is a big opportunity for high-impact outcomes by putting time into figuring out how to open up college resources and connectivity to flow back and forth between college and community.

However, no matter how logical this might sound, it's good to be sensitive to institutional and cultural barriers responsible for the typical suboptimal amount of college and local community connectivity. The history, structure, decision-making, and incentives within higher ed all feed into creating a more insular culture that puts any relationship development for students pointed exclusively toward faculty or alumni. There are few, if any, programs bringing students into contact with members of the local community not having an existing relationship with the college.

Sometimes a large local corporation might have some access or visibility, but rarely on a recurring program basis that would be open to a wide swath of colleges or community members.

Innovation-based companies will typically be earlier stage, moving fast, and not sufficiently resource-rich to devote management bandwidth toward developing college relationships. Even though they are ripe for bringing valued exposure to students, they won't be proactive in pursuing it, and colleges don't look at these companies as an attractive enough target to cultivate from their end.

Faculty or college administration also don't see it as their job to go out and develop new relationships in the community. Incentives for how they get paid or recognized for advancement within academia are simply not pointed in this direction.

Colleges also prefer to be at the physical center of any program. Since they have plenty of buildings, classrooms, and meeting spaces, the prevailing view is to expect people from the community to come on campus to take advantage of college-sponsored and -led programs.

But those in the community are not always so inclined to go on campus, particularly when it is located far from downtown, it has limited parking, finding a particular location is difficult, or they just don't like the idea of being spoon-fed from academia. While these objections don't apply to everyone, if they apply to some of the highly valued people a college could benefit from engaging, they are impediments that shouldn't be overlooked.

HOW TO WORK WITH HIGHER ED IN YOUR COMMUNITY

It's not enough for colleges to wait until their students approach graduation to help them get in contact with area alumni and other local resources about job opportunities. What I'm describing is a constant process throughout their education to help students get connected with the community at large.

While developing a broad range of supporting local relationships helps all students, its greatest job-generating impact will be for those aspiring to be entrepreneurs or team members in an innovation economy company.

Some colleges put on events, like pitch events, where students pitch ideas to a panel of successful entrepreneur alumni. These kinds of events encourage students to work together on pitch ideas, and also entice the university's celebrity entrepreneur alumni to connect with current students. It's absolutely worthwhile. However, it's only a small start.

Pitch events may form some loose connections, but since they are typically one-time events, they don't by themselves present the repeated interaction opportunities needed to foster relationship development beyond resources already affiliated with the college.

A simple variation of the pitch event approach is to do it off campus on some recurring basis, invite teams from other area colleges to participate in a coordinated event, and involve members of the local tech community to help prep the student pitchers.

TIPS FOR PITCH EVENT ORGANIZERS

I attended a local pitch event for the Upstate tech community that included four entrepreneurs pitching their startups. Like many other such events, the audience was a mixed group of entrepreneurs, community supporters, and a small handful of investors.

The pitches unfolded in typical fashion. When I saw the most common pitch errors across each of the four presenters, I wondered about how the event organizers went about setting expectations and guiding the entrepreneurs doing the pitching.

Entrepreneurs know these opportunities are important. They definitely spent time preparing, yet missed the chance to deliver a compelling case. Here are some suggestions to avoid the boring-pitch syndrome.

Tip #1: Problem and solution are not enough

Entrepreneurs (particularly those with a technical background) fall too easily into the trap of using precious minutes in a pitch to dumb down the science. They hope to wow the audience by spelling out the technical challenges that were overcome and the uniqueness of the founder's product design.

If half or more of the pitch is spent defining the scope of the startup's technology, it comes across like an academic exercise. The presenter is seen as working too hard to impress with his or her technical mastery—shortchanging the opportunity to secure support beyond defining problem and solution.

Tip #2: Pitch to investors, even in mixed groups

Even in situations where there is a mixed audience with diverse backgrounds and interests, I'm a fan of crafting pitches as if the entire audience were investors. Everyone wins by taking this approach in the pitch because:

- A standard set of guidelines can be provided to all presenters that directs them to a specific outcome
- The event can run on a consistent track, making it easier for the audience to compare pitches with a lens that helps everyone think about how investors look at whom to fund
- The entrepreneur gets an opportunity to further hone the investor pitch, addressing things like business model, channels of distribution, margins, and other critical business issues

Tip #3: Close with telling people what you want

I believe it's essential to end a pitch with a specific appeal for help. Oftentimes someone in the audience can assist the entrepreneur. The presenter just needs to ask!

Requests for help shouldn't be limited to financing. Telling people what else your startup needs right now gets everyone thinking about how and whom they know that can assist.

Whether it's introductions to a specific type of customer or channel partner, or finding new team members, mentors, and service providers, pitching is an opportunity to make a personal appeal. Someone in the audience may know the right resource for your company, but only if you tell them what you need.

Tip #4: Event organizers call the shots

With so many startups clamoring for the opportunity to get more exposure, event organizers have the leverage to set high standards for whom they choose to present. Instead of filling slots with whoever raises their hand first, consider inviting entrepreneurs to apply for the opportunity.

Even better, give them a short set of pitch guidelines on what you would like to see included in the pitch, and ask them to send a sample deck for you to evaluate. It's okay to tell applicants that their submission is just a sample. Ideally you and members of your supporting team can guide development of the final pitch so that it meets your target standard. Setting a high standard for your pitch events, and helping startup founders deliver compelling pitches will not only satisfy your audience, but reflect well on you as a sponsoring organization.

HELPING STUDENTS GET MORE CREATIVE COLLISIONS

It's easy to speak of deeper connections between students and the community, but what can we do to foster these connections? As I've written throughout this book, having recurring events with a diverse community audience that has reason to keep coming back is a way for people to interact multiple times, thus transitioning from one-time to repeated collision with the same people, thereby increasing the odds of getting true relationship development.

Jason Kuruzovich is an enterprising academic at Troy, New York–based Rensselaer Polytechnic Institute (RPI) who brought this to life well before he and I connected to work together on research leading to this book. With limited institutional support, Jason successfully launched and directed the Startup Tech Valley meetup group, now known throughout New York's Capital District area as SUTV (visit StartupTechValley. org). As a tenured professor at this premier technical university, Jason saw the outflow of RPI's strong talent, which included recent grads leaving Troy to start new companies in Boston, New York City, and Silicon Valley. He was already doing some mentoring on his own but wanted to increase his impact to reach a larger group than he could personally touch on his own.

We helped provide some input on the approach as well as some marketing support, but Jason took the reins in building an energized team of volunteers committed to working together to build a true community-wide recurring event that would spark creative collisions.

SUTV was novel to the Capital District because:

- It is held off campus in a downtown brew pub and event facility.
- It involves volunteers and participants from both academic and local business communities of the Capital District.
- It is marketed across several local colleges and business community networks.
- It features free admission, as event expenses are underwritten by sponsorships from multiple educational institutions, economic development organizations, and local businesses.
- It puts RPI students and teams on a level playing field with the rest of the community participants.

- It engages a combination of rookie and veteran entrepreneurs, investors, service providers in the tech community, and others simply interested in what's going on in the world of emerging tech.

SUTV's typical meeting agenda includes a very short welcome introduction, four pitches (with a short Q and A behind each pitch), community announcements, and brief closing remarks by a noted entrepreneur. Having that many speakers requires tight orchestration and clock management. The SUTV team doesn't hesitate to hook people off stage as they reach their specified time limit.

This also helps ensure adequate social time on both the front and back ends of the presentation segment, so everyone can mix with the speakers and each other, giving lots of opportunity for new creative collisions and/or catching up with someone met at a prior SUTV.

While we don't have stats on the number of companies spawned or resourced as a result of SUTV, we've certainly heard anecdotal evidence of people talking about important new relationships that got started as a direct result of SUTV interactions. In its fifth year, SUTV is still averaging two hundred to three hundred people per event, making it the most popular and highest-impact opportunity for creative collisions in the Capital District and attesting to the value this curated audience places on this type of recurring community-wide gathering.

Beyond aspiring entrepreneurs, these gatherings attract students looking for jobs with innovation economy companies and those who want to learn from like-minded people. The more exposure we can give these young people to connect with local entrepreneurs and other community resources, the more we can increase the odds those students start to feel the vibe of a supporting community by the time they graduate.

That's a winning model open to any college: bring students off campus and introduce them to the community of entrepreneurs and supporters in the local community. All parties are seeking exposure to new relationships that will help in their respective goals, and the college itself wins when these students expand their relationship network into the community.

LOOSENING THE TECH TRANSFER PROCESS

There is one additional form of potential interaction between colleges and the business community that is often squandered because of the college's island mindset.

Universities are incredible places for innovation, and their students create amazing breakthrough technological discoveries on a regular basis. These can be opportunities to partner with the business community in bringing new products to market. However, most colleges have amazing technological advances that nobody will ever use or even know about.

Why does this happen? Most university research is conducted by master's and PhD students under the guidance of faculty members. Once that research is complete, the university owns the results. Universities seek to commercialize the research results in an effort to earn back their investment. This approach makes sense in theory: the university does groundbreaking research, and local entrepreneurs can then buy their breakthrough technology, benefiting the larger community, including the university.

In practice, however, the majority of schools put so many hurdles in the way of licensing the technology that this rarely happens. Potential student entrepreneurs or others affiliated with the school look at the complicated tech transfer process and decide it's not worth the trouble.

On the other hand, some universities, such as Stanford and MIT, seem to consistently get their tech out into the world. They tend to have looser rules around their tech transfer practices. They might leave some money on the table because they don't play hardball with entrepreneurs who want to access their tech. But they have seen so much more gain in the long run that it baffles me that more colleges don't see the wisdom of a looser tech transfer approach.

Google is a perfect example. Google's technology was developed on the Stanford campus—using Stanford servers—while Larry Page and Sergey Brin were PhD students. When Larry and Sergey negotiated a tech transfer agreement, Stanford could have held firm, asking for big slices of Google's revenues going into the future. But administrators didn't. Stanford asked for nominal amounts in return for what it could have laid claim to, based on how university resources were used in the development of the initial product.

Stanford took the right path. They knew some portion of students experimenting like this would end up succeeding in ways that would truly be exceptional and they didn't want to slow that potential at the very critical early stages in converting research into a potentially commercial product. If the university provides a smooth and painless path to commercialization for students, and that tech leads to a massively successful company like Google, the entrepreneurs that created the company never forget where they came from. Between gains made from shares of Google stock (both from time of tech transfer and subsequent donations), we estimate the resulting impact for Stanford is now measured in the *billions*.

To fully utilize the talent on your community's campuses, campus leadership needs to understand that strict tech transfer regulations only inhibit the effort to build a stronger entrepreneurial community. Nobody knows which ideas will hit big and which ones will not. The more opportunities colleges give themselves to hit a home run, the more home runs they'll hit. The best way to do that is to loosen the rules and process around tech transfer and work harder at connecting the student entrepreneurs to resources in the community who can help them.

HOW TECH TRANSFER OFFICES CAN KILL STARTUPS

As an investor and board observer of a company in my UpVentures portfolio, I witnessed a painful tech transfer process this startup went through with a local university that ended up being very detrimental to its viability at a critical stage of the company's development.

The initial product vision arose from a graduate student's research, so he entered into discussion with the university's tech transfer department. The innovation was an energy-related technology that needed substantially more development beyond basic research to be market-ready. It would be a multiyear development cycle before it was compelling enough for the targeted original equipment manufacturers (OEMs) to integrate into their own supply chains and high-volume production processes.

In exchange for ownership of the initial research related intellectual property (IP), the entrepreneur negotiated a tech transfer agreement with what seemed like a reasonable arrangement, giving the university equity in the company, a small percentage of future revenues, and a cash payment of over $50,000 per year starting two years after signing the licensing agreement. It was the latter term that proved to be problematic.

As the startup continued its product development and discussions with OEMs, it quickly became apparent that the amount of research and development required to have something commercially viable was going to consume much larger amounts of capital than originally anticipated.

Even though the entrepreneur proved to be capital efficient, as the amount of outside investment grew, so did the impatience of the university to get some dollars from this cash-starved startup. The entrepreneur went to great lengths to share the reality of the company's situation and renegotiate the tech transfer terms to reflect the difficult position they were in. While it provided some minor accommodation on timing and amount of payment, the university took a hard line on getting paid, even though the company was both pre-revenue and burning substantial cash each month.

We investors balked at the notion of seeing our investment transferred to a university instead of undergoing the critical product development effort required to get the company to a revenue-generating stage. But when the university chose to initiate a formal claim against the startup demanding immediate payment, the CEO (with a reluctant board approving) paid the university to settle the claim.

It was clear the university's tech transfer department cared little about the potential for this company to succeed. Their own priorities seemed to be about the report card they were passing up to their bosses on how much cash was coming back from existing tech transfer agreements.

Notwithstanding promising newly developed IP and a path that investors supported, the company struggled after this incident, eventually shutting down, as it was not able to raise enough capital to continue the necessary product development for integrating its technology into the OEM supply chain. While the university's claim was not the defining reason for the company's demise, it was nonetheless indicative of how this particular school chose its internal priorities ahead of the bigger picture in supporting promising companies spinning out from academic research projects. News of these types of claims against startups rocket through both the entrepreneur and investor communities, providing additional reasons to avoid becoming involved with restrictive university tech transfer arrangements.

CORNELL ESHIP BEST PRACTICE EXAMPLE OF ENGAGING ENTREPRENEURIAL ALUMNI

Every school has a development department tasked with the mission of raising money from alumni. Within entrepreneurial circles, it is not uncommon to hear us talking about how the very business model of some schools seems to be grounded around their efforts to extract money from alumni!

That's in part due to the approach many schools take once they identify successful entrepreneur alumni, making repeated donation requests, typically for unrestricted use or with multimillion-dollar naming opportunities.

A common mantra in the nonprofit world is that if you want someone to become a donor, first find a path to get that person engaged in giving a slice of their time. Most universities don't seem to apply that philosophy, as the development offices treat all donors with the same general pitches and don't have the context or ability to figure out how to go about queueing up possible opportunities that could engage successful alumni entrepreneurs.

Over the years of our working with Cornell University, I've come to appreciate its winning approach as a counter to traditional university development and now hold it up as a best practice example. To begin with, Cornell has a dedicated eShip (entrepreneurship) team resourced and focused solely on developing and managing both recurring and multifaceted pathways that connect entrepreneurial students, Cornell alumni, and both university and community resources.

The Cornell eShip team manages an active and content-rich stream across several channels including traditional listservs, blogs, and college-wide communications, but also dedicated eShip event calendars, LinkedIn, Instagram, Facebook, Twitter, and YouTube channels. All of which make it more possible for someone to engage using an intake source that works best for them.

Generating an ongoing quantity of fresh content is not the work of a few, but instead the engagement of many, including students, faculty, alumni, and eShip community supporters. The small eShip team helps recruit volunteer content providers and manage input from multiple sources so the sum total of this rich content stream helps connect that segment of Cornell's far-flung alumni interested in entrepreneurship to adjust their intake to the amount and areas of interest to each individual constituent.

Instead of the development department beating on alumni to donate more, the eShip team identifies and establishes contact with entrepreneurial alumni to bring them into the communications loop and also find out what areas of the eShip program might be of interest to the alum.

Cornell's annual eShip celebration is a daylong affair that includes a symposium, various pitch event formats (accelerator demo day, *Shark Tank*–style on-the-spot deal-making, business plan/idea competition, etc.) and plenty of networking opportunities for alumni to mingle with student teams and each other.

The annual eShip Celebration draws more than seven hundred attendees, including students, faculty, alumni, investors, and community supporters. With more than half of the attendees being alumni, many are traveling in from outside the local community, in some cases even across the country.

eShip helped launch and manage eLab as a commercially operated off-campus coworking space that houses student teams working on innovative startups. eLab staff and local volunteer mentors help these teams get connected to the right resources spread around Cornell's eShip network.

One of the companies spun out of Cornell's eLab is StartupTree, a software-as-a-service that helps schools organize and engage their eShip resources. Cornell's eShip program was the pilot, and the platform is now in use at more than fifty colleges and universities across the United States (visit: Join.StartupTree. co). Cornell's eShip network also has points of presence with local events and networks in New York City and Silicon Valley that are managed with eShip staff resources.

While there aren't many schools that can match the size and scope of Cornell's Ivy League alumni base, it is important to remember that the school is located in a community of only thirty-one thousand people in a pretty isolated area of Upstate New York. Ithaca is a solid four-hour drive from New York City, and the closest city with 200,000 or more residents is two hours away.

Even though the vast majority of Cornellians immediately relocate upon graduation, Ithaca's burgeoning innovation economy has been stimulated by the collective efforts of Cornell eShip. Ithaca now has Upstate New York's fastest growth rate in tech employment and overall wage rate growth.

There were many people involved in growing eShip over the last eight years, probably none more impactful than Zach Shulman, a former Cornell professor who currently serves as both director of eShip and separately as general partner of Ithaca-based Cayuga Venture Fund mentioned in chapter 7. Zach's hands-on role as a professional early-stage venture investor, coupled with a keen sense of the academic landscape and an open-minded "give first" Silicon Valley ethos, gives some personal perspective we don't see often enough from leaders in academia.

As evidence of his outward-looking view, Zach has been on our Upstate Venture Connect board since we began and also serves on the board of Buffalo-based nonprofit Launch New

York, which is profiled in the next chapter. Both of these organizations contribute toward region-wide efforts to connect entrepreneurs to resources.

Learn more about Cornell's eShip by visiting eShip.Cornell.edu.

THE RIGHT PEOPLE FIND WAYS TO OVERCOME STIFLING UNIVERSITY BUREAUCRACY

When I started Upstate Venture Connect in 2010, I pursued an active outreach to speak with university presidents with hopes of raising their understanding about embracing opportunities that are now detailed in this book. I could pique their interest and sometimes got signals of their willingness to address challenges for their school to have a bigger impact on the local innovation economy while helping students and alumni at the same time.

Unfortunately, I found that enthusiasm from the top rarely translated to stimulating the necessary change to progress toward the outcomes we talked about. Part of the difficulty is due to the academic reward system being pointed in a very different direction, with no incentives in play to truly recognize faculty or staff who were in a position to make a difference.

Another factor was academia's consensus decision-making process at each level of a multitiered hierarchy. Good intentions from the top have a hard time filtering down to actual implementers who are needed to do the work.

We got lucky in finding Jim Joseph, dean of the Madden School of Business at Le Moyne College in Syracuse. While we had already begun a productive relationship with this Jesuit college through its current and prior presidents, as Jim came aboard with a CEO background and no encumbrances from a traditional academic career, he hit the ground running with his passion and get-things-done commitment to help us spread the reach and effectiveness of several programs, including the StartFast Venture Accelerator (hosted at Le Moyne College). UVC's partnership with Le Moyne has been multifaceted and instrumental in our spreading influence across Central New York.

Randy VanWagoner, president of Mohawk Valley Community College (mentioned in chapter 6 as a highly influential person), would be another example of an institutional leader who successfully fought through the challenges of academia to make a difference in stimulating the local innovation economy.

Randy first caught our attention when UVC started socializing the idea of a Mohawk Valley seed capital fund, described in chapter 7, as well as a collaborative effort among the area colleges for a possible college student incubator/accelerator and coworking facility. We did a series of small group luncheon meetings with community leaders and high-net-worth individuals who were potential investor candidates, and used those luncheons as a starting point to explain the job-generating aspects of a local innovation economy. Our discussions stood in sharp contrast to the prevailing political view of creating jobs with top-down, government-led, and taxpayer-funded initiatives.

Not only did Randy attend and begin absorbing this new viewpoint, he then opened up his personal network and started bringing high-profile alumni and others to these lunches, even though the discussion was not directly tied to a Mohawk Valley Community College–sponsored initiative.

Those discussions lead to a deeper exploration of a collaboration initiative involving the colleges in the area. After a couple of false starts with the local four-year colleges to lead the collaboration, Randy agreed to lead the effort and began the trek, resulting in the creation of the thINCubator, the Mohawk Valley's first incubator/coworking/events space dedicated to helping entrepreneurs launch companies both in the innovation economy and traditional small business (visit Thincubator.co).

thINCubator has an off-campus downtown location and serves as a community-wide facility that includes coordination with other local colleges and organizations. Now in its fourth year of operation, thINCubator has a robust menu of services and resources that are visible to area entrepreneurs to help them start and grow companies. Having a physical place that is a hub of innovation economy activity and events started raising community awareness, which in turn helped build support for us to take on even more ambitious projects to scale the community progress even faster.

Randy's leadership commitment and personal reputation in the community and broader circles were essential to navigating through the academia-related obstacles, including those imposed by the State University of New York system, of which MVCC is a part. But he also had a secret weapon we haven't seen at other colleges: a part-time director of development who was not an academic administrator or professional fundraiser, but instead an ultra-successful serial entrepreneur with a passion for helping his community.

Frank DuRoss is truly an entrepreneur's entrepreneur, having started thirty-four companies over the course of his career, about a half dozen of which are currently in operation in the local community. Understated, humble, and willing to give first are just some of Frank's personal qualities, consistent with the Silicon Valley ethos described in chapter 6. Frank gets things done and is very successful in getting others engaged to come on board to support high-impact initiatives that the college takes on, including those like thINCubator that don't fit in traditional boxes but are essential building blocks toward a job-generating local innovation economy.

FINDING DOERS WITH PASSION FOR INNOVATION ECONOMY

The task of guiding changes in the tech transfer process and curricula changes to become experiential and relevant for entrepreneurs will remain under the purview of the traditional academic hierarchy and thus it will be harder to stimulate change from the outside. But there are a host of other university-based resources that might be nudged into action if the right people are identified and engaged.

People like Jason Kurosovich, Zach Shulman, Jim Joseph, Randy VanWagoner, and Frank DuRoss make it possible to overcome common academia hurdles others say can't be crossed. It begins with their receptivity to new ideas, embracing perspective about the new economy future that's possible, and absolute commitment to actually do something about it, even if it means taking an unconventional route to get there.

Most importantly, it is this action bias I'll refer to as being a "doer" that matters.

I don't spend time pursuing the attention of university presidents anymore. But I am constantly searching the horizon to find other doers in academia without regard to what their formal role is. Prior business experience certainly helps, but a longer-term view, a track record of giving first, and evidence of crossing geographical and institutional boundaries in connecting others to get things done counts even more.

The only way to find these people is to go looking for them. I've found that visiting different events where college startup activity is taking place will uncover some through creative collision. Actively reaching out through my network to ask for a referral is another. But always with the qualifier of my looking for that doer.

And when we can connect these doers across geographical and institutional boundaries, a true network effect starts to emerge. That's when you know progress is on the path to start scaling with even greater impact.

SUMMARY

- Since the Retainment Quotient is such a crucial key to creating a Magnet City, higher ed has an important role to play if you are to increase the odds of keeping young talent local after they graduate.
- Higher ed can better prepare innovation economy workers by bringing more experiential learning into their programs—especially their entrepreneurship programs.

- The biggest thing that will lead to more students being retained in a Talent Exporting City is them being plugged into the local community through personal relationships that include HIPs.
- University programs can catalyze creation of local networks with recurring events that can also be off campus and marketed across the broader community.
- Pitch events can be one path to bring students and the local community together for sharing best practices and facilitating creative collisions.
- Many in higher ed have their own agendas, so it's important to find the right people who are already demonstrating by their actions that they aren't stymied by academic bureaucracy because they overcome hurdles to get things done for students and the community.

CHAPTER 9

ENGAGING NONPROFITS AND SOCIAL ENTERPRISES

HOW TO FIND AND COLLABORATE WITH SUPPORTIVE NONPROFITS

I don't care how much power, brilliance or energy you have, if you don't harness it and focus it on a specific target, and hold it there you're never going to accomplish as much as your ability warrants.

—ZIG ZIGLAR

My evolution into a mission-based fanatic about creating jobs has been largely through nonprofit roles. Not just because I serve as a volunteer; my path toward building a broad base of support began by growing several nonprofits from scratch that continuously chip away at the task of building collaborative relationships with other nonprofits who have charters for economic development or community-based philanthropy.

That nonprofit journey began as I was preparing to transition out of my role as TriNet's chairman and end my cross-country commute. The gradual descent from an active role in the company gave me freedom to start exploring ideas I had been kicking around in my head over all those years of cross-country flights.

The big break came in January 2009, when I attended an event orchestrated by the Upstate Capital Association, a nonprofit with members who are venture capital and private equity investors. It was at that meeting that I had my first visit to the Syracuse Tech Garden, an incubator buzzing with activity surrounding both young tech firm tenants and programs supporting the Syracuse tech community.

While I was impressed with what I saw, it was a creative collision meeting Nasir Ali, president of the Tech Garden, that became a seminal moment in drawing me toward the nonprofit path as the vehicle to start driving change by getting lots of other people involved.

We clicked immediately, as we saw common attributes in each other that we didn't find often enough in the Upstate region. Both of us had backgrounds as entrepreneurs with experience gained in markets elsewhere that were brimming with high-tech startups. We could see how Upstate had all the right assets to be a powerhouse in creating new tech companies, yet we were pragmatic in realizing the obstacles standing in the way of that happening here. But most importantly, it was our common commitment to both give first and play the long game that made our attraction mutual.

Nasir was a trailing spouse, having relocated in 2004 from Washington, DC, when his wife Uzma joined a large cardiology practice in Syracuse as partner. With experience as both a startup entrepreneur and professional management consultant with top national firms, he got snapped up by Syracuse Chamber of Commerce to launch the extensive retrofit of a ten-thousand-square-foot downtown parking garage to be repurposed as the Tech Garden.

By the time we met, the programs Nasir had developed were well underway, including the Seed Capital Fund mentioned in chapter 7. With the Tech Garden standing out as the jewel of high-tech community-building across all of Upstate, Nasir was active in his outreach to other Upstate tech resources and had a relationship network that spanned the entire region.

Since I was just beginning, our first efforts that year were to engage like-minded people from other communities who had roles in nonprofits that were actively involved in helping startups. We convened those startup ecosystem leaders several times over the course of that year, exploring paths to how we might share resources and collaborate. Since we were crossing both geographic and institutional boundaries to do so, this exploration was both unique and beneficial, setting the stage for the next move: Nasir and I co-founded nonprofit Upstate Venture Connect (UVC) in 2010, which became the basis for most of the content in this book.

While I provided UVC's startup capitalization and some ongoing support, our long-term success as a nonprofit public-benefit corporation only happened when there was enough recognition of the value we provide to have many others contributing financially in support of our mission.

This journey of building a sustainable nonprofit is something I continue to learn more about. It gives me appreciation for challenges faced by the many nonprofit partners we engage with.

ECONOMIC DEVELOPMENT ORGANIZATIONS

Several of those participants in the 2009 exploratory discussions remain in nonprofit leadership roles, still driving startup activity in their communities and now collaborating with UVC as we help spread connectivity throughout the region.

The Syracuse Chamber of Commerce merged with another local nonprofit economic development organization to become CenterState CEO, which continues running the Tech Garden as well as a range of other tech development programs and initiatives for a multicounty region. As explained in chapter 7, Rob Simpson, CenterState's forward-looking leader, was responsible for forging the collaboration that brought private-sector assets together to launch a professional venture capital firm, Armory Square Ventures.

Jim Senall runs NextCorps, a venture development nonprofit with a large incubator and an array of programs that build startup community. NextCorps originated with support rising out of public/private partnerships involving the University of Rochester and the local business community to advance high-tech company formation and talent engagement. The size and scope of programs expanded, with both public and private support, to now become a central hub of emerging tech across the Rochester metro area (visit NextCorps.org).

Marnie LaVigne, another early advocate going back to our 2009 exploratory meetings, went on to start Launch NY, today a high-impact nonprofit based in Buffalo (visit LaunchNY.org). Here is Launch NY's mission statement:

Launch New York, Inc. (Launch NY) is a 501(c)(3) venture development organization whose mission is to identify, support and invest in high-growth, high-impact companies and catalyze the entrepreneurial culture to drive job and wealth creation in the 27 westernmost counties of Upstate New York.

Launch NY delivers on this mission through a carefully constructed array of services that include mentoring by twenty entrepreneurs in residence (EIRs), connections to startup-relevant resources (including talent and early-stage funding sources), and events and communications for entrepreneurs and startup company leadership, to name just a few.

The wide geography covered by Launch NY puts it in a unique position compared to most single-community-oriented economic development nonprofits. That heightens its need to get others involved in supporting its mission by constantly expanding whom they touch outside the Buffalo home base to engage those geographically dispersed contacts in helping fill needs across the entire network.

Another impressive Launch NY accomplishment has been the steady march in building funding sources to not only support its EIR-centric delivery model, but also seed capital for investing in companies it serves.

Beginning with grants from both public and private sources, a philanthropy-sourced seed fund makes investments in the range of $25,000 to $100,000 for companies that are typically pre-revenue or early-stage revenue, yet have advanced to show some level of customer engagement. The availability of this funding source acts as a carrot for startups to work with Launch NY's EIRs, providing further insights on which startup leaders are coachable and show promise of building a scalable company.

Startups showing promise following that initial seed round can then apply to get linked into Launch NY's investor network for a larger round, which may include participation from a for-profit fund that Launch NY is setting up at time of this publication.

Any investment gains realized from startups participating in the original Launch NY seed fund round are returned to the fund for reinvestment in other startups.

Investment gains realized by the for-profit fund will be returned to the participating limited partner investors with a carried-interest portion (profit realized after limited partners have had their capital returned) kept by Launch NY to cover its administration and management expenses in running the fund.

Building the relationships that led to raising the funding for Launch NY's services and seed funding was a Herculean effort entirely attributable to the vision and perseverance of CEO Marnie LaVigne. This was not a "get one big check" kind of build, but rather a series of incremental steps forging a coalition of public and private funders to participate with multiyear commitments.

PHILANTHROPIC SUPPORT FOR JOB CREATION

Each of these ecosystem-building nonprofits had some level of contribution from philanthropic sources. It's worthwhile to dive into that as a separate category of potential support.

Launch NY got off the ground with initial support from Buffalo's John R. Oishei Foundation. As the delivery model started showing traction, the foundation was joined by several other philanthropies, including large grants from the Ralph C. Wilson, Jr. Foundation. These foundations, and others supporting the named nonprofits, all had one thing in common: they were founded by very successful entrepreneurs who cared about their communities.

Both John Oishei and Ralph Wilson have long since passed, but their foundation charters left sufficient visibility for successor trustees to expand beyond the traditional support of community needs in education, human services, arts, health, etc., and recognize that if a community is to thrive, it has to have a growing private-sector-led economic base that creates jobs.

Marnie had interactions with Oishei Foundation board members and got them engaged with some of her entrepreneur-supporting activities as part of the University of Buffalo Center for Bioinformatics. As the relationships deepened, it took time to develop and nurture a plan that aligned with the respective foundation charters and her vision of a sustainable entrepreneur-support organization for Western New York's innovation companies.

Community foundations would be another philanthropy vehicle to consider. These nonprofits aggregate many local donors into a larger, professionally managed operation that helps identify and curate local charitable needs, and administer grants on behalf of their participating donors. The community foundation model is particularly appealing to donors who want to direct charitable contributions toward the community but want to do so with some professional staff and governance that the individual donor may lack on their own.

Community foundations are great organizations to look into, since their board members are frequently leaders in the community who might fit the highly influential person profile. That said, many community foundations are oriented toward the traditional philanthropy categories of education, human services, health, arts, recreation, etc., so while their relationship value is high, we've found their pathway as a funding source will largely depend on the openness of their leadership to seeing that the connection between private-sector job growth and a healthy community is within their charitable aim.

The best community foundation leaders are those thinking long-term in realizing that their current donor base is destined to shrink because they're in a Talent Exporting City. Whether due to deindustrialization, closure of a large military base, or some other game-changing economic factor, flight of the area's best talent also means the future of their community foundation is on the decline.

Our superstar leader in this category is Alicia Dicks, CEO of the Community Foundation of Herkimer and Oneida Counties, an organization with about $150 million in assets making $8 million-plus per year in grants. Unusual for a philanthropy executive, her prior background was more in business development roles in private-sector organizations. But she is also an entrepreneur on the side, co-owning a successful restaurant and married to another local entrepreneur who has a visible and active role in the community. All of these vantage points led to Alicia's appreciation for the problems faced in Utica/Rome and Mohawk Valley and for the mission of the two-county community foundation.

When her board member Randy VanWagoner, president of Mohawk Valley Community College, started talking up a vision for what was to become the thINCubator (described in chapter 8), Alicia not only helped build funding support through the foundation, but also helped engage other members of her board to become active in the efforts growing the Mohawk Valley's nascent startup ecosystem. More recently, as we helped introduce the Innovation Collective initiative, described below, Alicia was a key HIP, bringing others into the fold with her advocacy for this truly "build from the bottom up" approach, so very different from the expected path to build a jobs-generating community.

SOCIAL ENTERPRISES SUPPORTING ECOSYSTEM GROWTH

Social entrepreneurship is an emerging trend, with companies being founded based on a purpose-driven social mission for developing and implementing solutions addressing a specific societal, cultural, or environmental issue.

Starting as a company generally excludes a social enterprise from receiving grants reserved for nonprofits, so it's a tall order to create a sustainable value proposition with limited opportunities to attract investor capital.

As with any startup, overcoming the significant hurdles to become sustainable requires that social enterprises be piloted by entrepreneurs with a passionate commitment to develop and implement solutions targeting a specific problem that customers are willing to pay them for.

Innovation Collective (IC) is a social enterprise based in Coeur d'Alene, Idaho, that we've engaged as part of our ecosystem building effort in Utica, New York. We were attracted by Innovation Collective's proven formula for building startup community from the bottom up by finding and empowering people who might be overlooked and disconnected. IC engages people by helping them set personal goals and pursue targeted development within IC's defined framework, leading to entrepreneurship or joining others working on initiatives that appeal to the individual's personal passion (visit Innovation-Collective.co).

Getting community buy-in to contract with IC as an out-of-state social enterprise was an effort in itself that is profiled in chapter 10: Engaging Government.

OHUB POWERS AN EQUITABLE INNOVATION ECOSYSTEM

Opportunity Hub (OHUB) is an Atlanta-based social enterprise with a mission to create racial equity in the tech, startup, and venture ecosystem. Founded by Rodney Sampson, OHUB began as a startup incubator intentionally focused on increasing diversity, equity and inclusion through a structured program that combines instruction, mentoring, and connecting talent to opportunities.

OHUB's first seventy-five-hundred-square-foot campus in downtown Atlanta was launched in 2013. The organization has since added fourteen thousand square feet with expansion to Atlanta's West Midtown Giant Lofts and then partnered with some local entrepreneurs and venture capitalists to open a twenty-five-thousand-square-foot campus in Georgia Tech's Technology Square. That partnership has invested in over forty high-growth tech startups that have raised more than $400 million in follow-on capital, are valued at US$1.5 billion and employ more than two thousand people. OHUB also operates facilities in Kansas City, Missouri, and on the campus of Morehouse College in Atlanta, Georgia.

Bringing people into place-based facilities for OHUB programs is just the starting point. OHUB has steadily grown pathways for socially disadvantaged communities via its online webinars and portal, skills training, and early job placement programs powered by its income-sharing agreement fund, startup entrepreneurship support programs and accelerators, and capital formation initiatives via 100 Black Angels and Allies Fund I.

With OHUB's concentrated focus on lifting up those in minority and disadvantaged communities, the combination of various OHUB programs has resulted in growing an extensive network of talent that is now highly sought after by companies seeking to expand their diversity, equity, and inclusion.

At the time of publication, we are in active discussion with OHUB to explore collaborative opportunities to leverage its resources as an avenue to accelerate our region's outreach and engagement for diversity, inclusion, and racial equity (visit OpportunityHub.co).

DEVELOPING PRODUCTIVE NONPROFIT RELATIONSHIPS

Finding the right nonprofits to develop relationships with is a process in itself. My estimate is that for every productive relationship with a nonprofit, I probably touched twenty others that didn't pan out. Like a lot of things in the world of pursuing causes we're passionate about, we have to be willing to take many shots on goal in order to see a few eventually find their way into the net.

The easiest ones to locate, and probably the most receptive, will be those that already have some kind of connection to the startup world. They might be local community–focused, or perhaps have a larger mandate, like Upstate Capital Association, responsible for the event where I had my "aha!" collision with UVC co-founder Nasir Ali.

But there is much to be done with nonprofits outside of the startup space, like economic development–oriented nonprofits or especially philanthropic funding sources. However, these areas require much more research and willingness to go and meet people, perhaps colliding with them at events where they would be hanging out.

I was fortunate to be able to operate under the umbrella of nonprofit Upstate Venture Connect, which helped open some doors since I had a verifiable reason to engage other nonprofit leaders. Then it was up to me to ascertain their interest and suitability to help develop their thinking to a direction they might not have given much thought to before.

Rarely was there an instant connection that evolved into immediate collaboration. Instead there had to be mutual interest in wanting to invest in building the relationship, with both parties seeing value in doing so.

If I could see the potential fit, then I would be thinking, "What do I have to offer that can help this nonprofit?" If I had learned enough about their current priorities and challenges, perhaps there was someone I had in my resource network who could be the right person, as a service provider, donor, board member, public official, or other resource, to address one of their identified needs.

Could I attract the nonprofit (NP) executive to attend a startup community event to get a feel for what was going on outside their view? Was there a startup or successful innovation economy company right in their community that would be of interest for them to know about?

These are just a few of the questions I would be asking myself in the search for how I might give first.

When I reflect on common threads through the highest-value NP relationships that developed, I find it still came down to being much more tied to the personal qualities of the individual than the nature of the NP's charter and constituency. Almost all NP execs are mission- and community-oriented, but it's a smaller subset who are forward-looking enough to go outside the box of traditional nonprofit approaches and thinking to be receptive toward differences involved in the world of innovation economy.

It's no coincidence that Nasir, Marnie, and Alicia's backgrounds as entrepreneurs also influenced their views on the challenges faced by those starting companies.

As with all of our most productive collaborative relationships, evidence of a person's willingness to cross geographic and institutional boundaries to get things done instantly piques my interest to see how I might pursue getting them engaged. Especially if I sense that give first attitude and curiosity about how the innovation economy connects with their world.

I'll put them on the cultivate list and circle back for periodic touches, including meetings when I've uncovered something that may offer a resource appropriate for one of their needs. Keeping the highest-value targets warm is a part of being in sales, something that definitely carries over from the business side of entrepreneurship to build successful, productive relationships with nonprofit people who can make a difference.

When I bring up the role of nonprofits in helping to build a strong local economy, startup founders often have adverse reactions. They've experienced some bureaucracy or frustration in partnering with nonprofits in the past and they jump to conclusions, losing respect for the nonprofit world as a whole.

As a result, nonprofits are an often-overlooked resource on our journey to create more good jobs in our community. The reality is that nonprofits are interested in creating the same kind of thriving community that you are—they just have different perspectives and different sets of resources. They can be incredible partners.

WHY WORK WITH NONPROFITS?

Say the word *nonprofit* and you'll often see a glaze form over the eyes of an entrepreneur. Nonprofits have a reputation (not necessarily deserved) for moving slowly, being poorly run, and putting lots of red tape in the way of getting things done.

The greatest reason to collaborate with nonprofits is that they are mission-driven organizations. Whereas businesses are always balancing their mission with their profits and individuals are balancing their mission with their own needs, nonprofits exist for the mission they serve. As a result, it is easy to identify nonprofits that align deeply with what you are trying to accomplish.

Although there is sometimes friction between nonprofits (which I discuss below), the best nonprofits are not competitive. They are focused on achieving a certain outcome and happy to collaborate in furthering a shared mission.

Compared to businesses and individuals, nonprofits tend to be less concerned with getting their piece of the pie, and far more concerned with producing an impact. This makes them great partners. As long as you can avoid internal politics, you can become sufficiently aligned to collaborate in helping your community thrive.

Beyond the immediate support they can provide, nonprofits also provide a great deal of legitimacy for your cause. Nonprofits are often well-known and respected in the community, and partnering with nonprofits allows some of that credibility to rub off on your cause.

Sadly, people often assume the worst when entrepreneurs get together to work on a new project, such as building an entrepreneurial community. They might assume that you have selfish motivations and ask, "What's in it for you?" But when people see that you're working for a larger vision across multiple organizations, including nonprofits and their leaders, it dissolves this suspicion. With the seal of approval from a nonprofit, people are more likely to trust that you're focused on the greater good, and therefore more likely to donate their time, talent, and treasure to support your cause.

Most importantly, nonprofits present an opportunity to connect with more individuals who can support your cause. Working with nonprofits, you'll meet a wide range of people who are passionate about solving society's challenges.

As I've described, the best way to accomplish change is to get the right people on board, and nonprofits present a great way to find the people who have the resources, connections, and desire to help improve your community.

The first place we look is the nonprofit's board of directors. A good nonprofit will have an active board that includes entrepreneurs. Quite often, the entrepreneurs on nonprofit boards don't have a background in innovation industries. They might come from banking or healthcare, or they could be attorneys or real estate developers. These are successful people in our community who clearly care about giving back, and they can be great resources.

Nonprofits also have mission-driven people on their staff and donor lists full of wealthy people who care about making an impact. The right nonprofits are like magnets for the types of people we want to be surrounded by on this journey.

WHICH ORGANIZATIONS SHOULD YOU PARTNER WITH?

Not every nonprofit is a potential partner. Choose selectively which organizations align with the mission you are on and have the best ability to support you.

To start, focus on organizations that are involved in economic development. Clearly, an organization that is dedicated to providing clean drinking water in developing nations isn't likely to be a great supporter of your work in building an entrepreneurial economy. Your goal isn't to change the fundamental mission of any organization you work with—it's to find the nonprofits that are already most aligned with your goals and build relationships with them.

More specifically, be on the lookout for nonprofits that are tightly aligned with your mission and already focused on job creation *beyond training*. These are sometimes called venture development organizations, and they usually have a mission that focuses on fostering entrepreneurs to help them connect to resources in newer industries.

The most crucial component of making a good match is that they have a similar perspective to you on how to accomplish this mission. In my experience, many nonprofits in Talent Exporting Cities think the best way to create jobs is to recreate the industrial era. They don't understand the shift toward innovation economy jobs. Although their goals are similar, their means of achieving those goals will look radically different from yours.

For example, in Upstate New York, the residue of an industrial economy is everywhere. As a result, people in nonprofits try to raise a lot of money and attention to create manufacturing jobs. I don't have to tell you twice: manufacturing jobs are not the future for our next generation. Find nonprofits where leadership embraces the notion of learning and collaboration, and understands how innovation economy jobs lead to more good jobs for everyone.

Once you've done all that, ensure that they prioritize the mission over their politics. Although that should be how every nonprofit operates, some NP execs talk a nice game but take actions reflecting a zero-sum-game mentality. These execs see others who are trying to accomplish the same goal as their competition and they zoom in narrowly on the accomplishments that are theirs, versus those that belong to others.

This often stems from a scarcity mentality, in which they see potential collaborators as competitors and feel the need to show their own accomplishments in a narrowly defined way to impress their donor base. If they see their job as catering to their funding sources rather than serving their mission, then they are really just a business that happens to earn their income from donations. As a result, you'll never be able to work together effectively.

The nonprofits you're looking for won't see other businesses and nonprofits as competition, but rather as potential collaborators. With this mindset, they will be happy to spill their efforts and resources across boundaries. They understand that a rising tide lifts all boats, even if the boats aren't in the same ZIP code. These are the organizations that will be willing to think on a larger scale and work together to accomplish their mission, even if the specifics are outside the scope of their usual work.

To truly assess this flexibility, we take time to figure out where a particular nonprofit gets its funding. Certain sources of funding come along with requirements that initially drive the NP executive to see that zero-sum-game picture and become difficult to collaborate with.

As an example, government grants usually are earmarked to address a specific social objective, such as helping women or improving minority-owned businesses. Those are valid and worthy causes, but by serving only that specific social need in a targeted area, their efforts become constrained. They can only use their money and time for that one purpose. Generally, there are too many strings attached to the government money behind public nonprofits, and the more strings attached to an organization, the less room the organization has to take the risks that are necessary to succeed.

An unwillingness to take risks or see the bigger picture goes directly against everything we are discussing. For nonprofits to succeed in accomplishing the type of change described in this book they have to work across boundaries, whether they're geographic, mission-based, or generational. Government-backed nonprofits with straightjacketed constraints won't be able to cross those boundaries.

This brings us to the most important aspect to consider in evaluating nonprofits: the people. If we see the leader of a nonprofit crossing institutional (or, even better, geographic) boundaries, we know we've found someone who is more focused on the mission than on their charter or funding source.

Even if some organizations have a narrow focus, if we can find the innovative people within these organizations, there will be room to work together. On close inspection, sometimes the perceived constraints from funding sources disappear and our two nonprofits are on a path to collaboration.

Unfortunately, the residual effects of industrial success in our past leads to many nonprofits not meeting the above criteria. The nonprofits that are stuck in the past will be less likely to venture out to events like tech meetups and entrepreneur pitch events. Engaging in those activities would help push the nonprofit leader beyond their self-imposed boundaries. Those who aren't constrained by these boundaries, real or imagined, are the ones we want to spend more time seeking out or nurturing.

HOW TO INTERACT WITH NONPROFITS

As discussed in part 2, all the relationships we build as we develop a community culture fostering successful entrepreneurship should start with a give first mentality. The relationships we form with nonprofits should be no different.

Giving is the language of nonprofits. As we build our relationships with them, we focus first on what we can give them. We look at their mission, their budget, the size of their network, and their donor list. Where do they need help? We don't necessarily have to give the nonprofit target any of our limited financial resources, but we can *put them in contact with people* who will. We ask ourselves who we know that could further that nonprofit's mission, improve their bottom line, grow their network, or join their list of regular donors.

In return, they may share their resources with us. Or they may not; that's fine too! We give from a place that expects nothing in return. That's the culture we want to be building in our community, and our job is to lead by example.

When we identify an individual in the nonprofit world we believe is worth cultivating a relationship with, we focus on bringing them value in a way that's aligned with both of our missions. We're ready for the long haul, because nonprofits and the people who serve them aren't generally eager to jump into risky opportunities. That's not their wheelhouse. It might take years, but the right person is worth the effort.

One approach to start deepening relationships with nonprofit leaders is by encouraging them to attend our community events so they can personally get a feel for the people involved in the innovation economy companies and supporters. The nonprofit world tends to be wary of entrepreneurs, so the more of a chance they get to see what you are building, the more they can understand that our missions are aligned.

The right nonprofit leader might also be a candidate to speak at one of the startup community events. This has potential to be a win-win scenario. For the nonprofit leader, speaking to a group of entrepreneurs gets their message out in front of more people and builds support in the community. From your perspective, you are getting a chance to expose this leader to the entrepreneurial community and develop empathy for the needs and perspectives of entrepreneurs.

Nonprofit relationships take a long time to cultivate, but building an innovation economy community is a long-term endeavor, and expanding your network out to nonprofits is worth the effort. Give them the opportunity to join you on your mission, and in the end, you'll both end up better off for it.

SUMMARY

- Nonprofits are incredible potential partners because they are mission-driven, so making an impact is their main focus.
- Nonprofits can help by providing legitimacy, funding, and connections.
- Get to know local nonprofits with overlapping missions to yours, and work (with a give first mentality) to support one another.
- There can be a lot of politics in the nonprofit world, so be sure to focus your energy on relationships with those who are truly in service of their mission and not territorial.

CHAPTER 10

ENGAGING GOVERNMENT

HOW TO ADVOCATE FOR JOB-CREATING POLICIES AND RESOURCE ALLOCATION

Instead of focusing on [those] circumstances that you cannot change, focus strongly and powerfully on the circumstances that you can.

—JOY PAGE

If you think sustainable growth in good jobs is going to come from the government, I have some bad news for you: it's not (and you haven't been paying a lot of attention to this book so far).

Federal, state, and local governments all have incredible power to shift resources, incentivize actions, and convene decision-makers to get things done. Politicians can be influential allies in the mission to revitalize our communities. But in their core role, government officials aren't the people who create private-sector companies that grow good jobs—that's what entrepreneurs do.

Since the launch of the nonprofit Upstate Venture Connect in 2010, my own focus has been all about engaging private-sector resources to support first-time entrepreneurs in the newer industries. UVC purposely steered clear of pursuing government grants and support, as the very nature of what we do just doesn't line up with the prevailing view of how governments go about economic development.

But in 2016, I veered head-on into the world of politics by making the decision to run for federal office in New York's 22nd congressional district. My friends and colleagues were more than a little surprised, since my private-sector orientation and preference for being behind the scenes seemed so at odds with all that would be involved in taking on a very public and consuming campaign effort.

Adding to their incredulity was my choice to run as an independent candidate on a new ballot line we created called the Upstate Jobs Party. All of us were very well aware that no one had been elected to Congress as a third-party candidate since Bernie Sanders in 1990.

Yes, it's okay to call me a bit crazy. Certainly, I was passionate enough about the journey to help others create companies and jobs that I saw the congressional campaign as a supreme opportunity to learn about the world of politics and public policy. I also knew that my campaign would be a chance to build a broader base of support for others to see there are more paths to job creation than what our politicians talk about.

Our campaign made huge strides, and by the end of September 2016, independent polling confirmed I was trending toward striking distance of the margin of error of being tied with the two major party candidates. We had enough traction that we garnered national press citing NY-22 as the only race in the country where an independent candidate had a shot at winning,[14] and I was the only third-party candidate for Congress to ever be endorsed by the US Chamber of Commerce.[15]

There's certainly a lot of drama behind how we went from there to being crushed on election day, as well as the continuing journey to build the Upstate Jobs Party as a political force (visit UpstateJobs.org). While it's interesting enough to fill another book, I'll limit my comments in this chapter to a few key observations about government and how to advocate to public officials that are now influenced by my having been in the trenches of the political process and a continuing journey to articulate these themes to the public at large.

CAN GOVERNMENT CREATE JOBS?

Most people see that there is a role for the government to help shape the environment that is conducive to growing jobs.

Too often the general public discussion about government is limited to policy themes like lowering taxes and reducing restrictions on business. While I support those goals, I would note that states that might lay claim to already having low taxes and being business-friendly don't always line up as job-generating machines in the newer industries.

In fact, if you analyze markets with the highest rates of new industry and overall job growth—such as Silicon Valley, South-

---

14   "Martin Babinec In The News," *Babinec for Congress*, http://babinecforcongress.com/category/media/page/3/.

15   Mark Weiner, "Syracuse.com: A First—US Chamber of Commerce Backs Independent in Upstate NY House Race," Babinec for Congress, October 18, 2016, http://babinecforcongress.com/us-chamber-backs-independent-in-upstate-ny-house-race/.

ern California, New York City, Boston, Seattle, and Washington, DC metro—you'll find that these areas have some of the highest tax rates and/or the most business-unfriendly regulations in the country.

People consistently overestimate the role of lower taxes and lower regulations in building an entrepreneur-friendly community and underestimate the importance of the other factors I've described in earlier chapters, such as facilitating connections and finding early-stage capital for new entrepreneurs.

Although it's not necessary to gain favor from local and state politicians in order to build a thriving local community, politicians have immense power to bring about some changes and help convene the right people to support a community-wide job-creation effort. But to engage public office–holders and others in government it is helpful to first understand how they look at economic development and find paths that align with their own interests.

WHAT SHOULD POLITICIANS AND GOVERNMENT AGENCIES DO INSTEAD?

Our premise is that growth in good jobs best comes by accelerating the number of entrepreneurs creating companies in the newer industries, and the most important factor in the success of these new entrepreneurs is driving the right connections to others who can help them on their journey.

With this understanding in mind, the role of government becomes clear: to make policies and resource allocations addressing unique needs of innovation entrepreneurs without having to spend boatloads of taxpayer money. And for individual politicians, to be aware that their office brings potential to convene highly influential people, getting them off the sidelines and into the game of helping the next generation of company-builders.

All of this begins by having politicians better understand the needs of startups. Most politicians still equate startups with small businesses, which then leads into the trap of applying traditional small business programs and tactics.

That approach isn't suitable for startups that face very different challenges and different realities than traditional small businesses. As I've described in our opening chapters, a startup is either building an innovative new product in a new market, or a new product in an existing market. In either case it requires a paradigm shift on the part of the customer who will be buying the startup's product. Hence you have a bigger investment required to not just develop the innovation, but also go through the iterative process of finding "product-market fit," then scale up the company with bigger investments in sales and marketing than what can be fueled by incremental growth in new customer sales.

The startup's biggest resource handicap is finding growth capital sufficient to draw talented people whose skills are in great demand and can work anywhere. Startups can't go to a commercial bank and get a loan—they need private investment capital.

When meeting with a public official who I think can help, I'll typically take time to unpack the differences between small businesses and startups, then transition to why startups drive the 5 to 1 job multiplier described in chapter 1 that small businesses, traditional services, or even manufacturing won't achieve. Depending on the flow of discussion, I'll also try to work in elements of the virtuous cycle of good jobs described in part 1 of the book.

With an understanding of these themes, my focus will be to encourage government officials to support these efforts through public policy and resource allocation, as well as by taking advantage of the politician's power to convene.

Let's begin with a few policy opportunities. Some of these are state or municipal level; others may be big-picture federal but can help paint the picture of the kind of policies that we entrepreneurs think could help influence the creation of more good jobs.

PUBLIC POLICIES THAT WOULD HELP STARTUPS
POLICY: TAX INCENTIVES ENCOURAGING INDIVIDUALS TO INVEST IN STARTUPS

As outlined in chapter 7, one of the most important components of a thriving local startup community is the availability of early-stage private capital. Strategies described in that chapter show how anyone can help encourage those with financial capacity to get off the sidelines and into the game of helping the next generation of company-builders.

While I'll reiterate that personal contact in getting individuals to participate is the most effective path to get capital to early-stage companies, the supporting policy approach I advocate would be tax incentives encouraging individuals to save on ordinary income or capital gains taxes as the result of their investing in startup companies.

Targeting individual investors is most beneficial because this is the funding source most likely to participate in supporting earlier-stage companies that are not advanced enough to attract institutional capital from professional investors such as venture capital firms.

A variety of investor tax incentive policies have been tried in various states. Nonprofit Angel Capital Association (visit AngelCapitalAssociation.org) cites Wisconsin and Ohio as states with angel-friendly policies that have produced significant growth in early-stage investor participation.

Sometimes a state might have a startup incentive policy in place that investors don't even know about. I discovered this after taking a meeting with my New York state senator, seeking input on job creation. In a visit to my home he asked, "Martin, what kind of policy would help us get more angel investments into startups here?" Instead of giving a flip answer on the spot, I offered to do some research to look at best-practice examples and come back with recommendations for incentives comparing New York to other states.

Even though I was one of Upstate New York's most active early-stage investors, prior to my being asked for this input, I wasn't knowledgeable of an existing New York State angel investor incentive I was eligible for. Lo and behold, after doing the research, I was more than a little surprised to figure out New York State actually had a pretty decent tax credit for angel investing in startups already on the books!

New York State has a statute defining a qualified emerging technology company (QETC), which is a reasonably good definition of a startup fitting the innovation economy companies we've talked about throughout the book. For the companies that apply to be certified as QETCs, both the company and its qualifying angel investors are eligible to receive sufficient tax credits to be worth the effort of going through the certification process.

In peeling back how we missed that (as did the CEOs of twenty-plus New York State startups in my portfolio at the time), it was clear that the absence of any government resources being devoted to the policy's implementation left it languishing with no visibility or staff to support even basic inquiries about how to qualify for the incentive, and thereby the policy missed the opportunity to make a difference in fueling private capital into early-stage companies.

A sad footnote to this experience is that five years after submitting a paper summarizing my findings and recommendations through appropriate channels, and multiple interactions with public officials that included testifying on the subject before the New York State Assembly, no action has been taken to increase the visibility or accessibility of this existing incentive.[16] So New York State startup companies and investors both miss out because no one knows about an existing incentive already in statute and available to them.

POLICY: RESTRICT NONCOMPETE AGREEMENTS

Noncompete agreements might seem like an inconsequential and esoteric problem to focus on as you build a startup-friendly environment, but they're surprisingly important. As individuals jump from job to job within the tech sector—and eventually start their own businesses—their noncompete agreements with former employers become a burden on the free movement of labor. Multiply that burden across hundreds of thousands

---

16 "Martin Babinec Testimony to NYS Assembly," Upstate Jobs Party, November 13, 2017, https://upstatejobs.org/martin-babinec-testimony-nys-assembly/.

of people in innovation economy jobs and you'll see that non-compete agreements dramatically slow down the growth of the local economy.

How can we avoid this? Courts and public policy in California take the position that noncompete agreements are not enforceable, effectively making them useless. That is one of the few things California public policy has done that has contributed significantly to the growth of Silicon Valley and innovation statewide.

State governments are not incentivized to make this change, even after hearing arguments about how restricting noncompetes would be like putting grease in the wheels of the free flow of labor, allowing workers to go where they can have the highest impact.

Like many things affecting public policy, the forces with the money to invest in candidates and lobbying are organized and benefit from the status quo. There is no coalition representing the rights of workers to go unrestricted into their next opportunity.

Restricting noncompete agreements will not only attract more talent to your state and community, but also allow workers to consistently find the best opportunities, which is a win for everyone.

POLICY: MORE IMMIGRATION OPPORTUNITIES FOR WORKERS WITH VALUED SKILLS

Although much of the national discussion of immigration revolves around the battle over people flowing across the southern border, this dialogue misses a crucial fact: there is a category of immigrants who actually create jobs.

The National Foundation for American Policy (NFAP) reports that immigrants have started more than half (fifty of ninety-one) of America's startup companies valued at $1 billion or more and are key members of management or product development teams in more than 80 percent of these companies.

NFAP research finds that these immigrant-founded billion-dollar-plus startup companies have created an average of twelve hundred jobs per company and have an aggregated value of $248 billion, an amount which is more than the total value of all the companies listed on the public stock exchanges of countries like Ireland, Argentina, and Portugal.[17]

Keep in mind, the companies mentioned here are only the highly visible segment of startups rising to the "unicorn" level of $1 billion or more in valuation. For each unicorn there are thousands of smaller companies in earlier stages that are well below the radar from a tracking perspective, yet likely have a greater number of employees in the aggregate than the total employment of the unicorns.

So as we continue the immigration policy discussion, with the number of people wanting to come here far outstripping our capacity to absorb them, it only makes sense to be looking at ways we might get more of the right immigrants, having higher potential to actually contribute to creating jobs.

---

17   Stuart Anderson, "Immigrants and Billion-Dollar Companies," National Foundation for American Policy, October 2018, https://nfap.com/wp-content/uploads/2018/10/2018-BILLION-DOLLAR-STARTUPS.NFAP-Policy-Brief.2018.pdf.

STARTUP VISA

With input from passionate people in startup entrepreneurship circles, the Obama administration used powers of the executive branch
to create a program called Startup Visa to harness the opportunity
presented by immigrant entrepreneurs, particularly in the innovation economy. The Startup Visa program defined standards and a
process to determine who could qualify as company founders to
stay in the country while building a business. Sadly, as details of the
program administration were worked out in the final portion of the
Obama term, just as it was ready to start processing applications,
the Trump administration came aboard and decided to cancel the
program.

There remain many advocates for the Startup Visa program, including bipartisan support in Congress, but it will be held hostage in the
overall immigration policy debate due to differing views on whether
smart policies like Startup Visa should be passed piecemeal versus
the current path of being held up to become part of one big omni-
bus immigration policy package.

Even though the quagmire in updating the broken federal immigration policy is likely to be with us for some time, there is an innovation
we can point to at a state level that appears to offer a promising
pathway for talented immigrant entrepreneurs to remain in country
while proceeding through the lengthy process of qualifying under
current immigration policies.

Massachusetts created the Global Entrepreneur in Residence (GEIR)
program for immigrants who graduated from a US university or par-
ticipated in a US acceleration/incubation program. They must have
an incorporated and financed startup. They can then apply for a
university-sponsored visa that allows the entrepreneur to remain in

country while their startup grows to qualify as a sponsoring company under the existing federal H-1B visa rules.

Since launching the program in 2014, 110 initial (H-1B) and follow-on visas (O-1, EB-1) have been approved, for a success rate of 100 percent. The entrepreneurs' companies in this program have 940 employees and have raised more than $500 million in venture capital.[18]

The GEIR program was spearheaded by MIT and other top universities in Massachusetts and raised initial program funding from the private sector through a coalition of successful entrepreneurs and service providers actively engaged in the startup community. States with high participation of immigrant students in universities featuring strong STEM programs would be the best fit for such a program— but only if there are other elements of a supporting ecosystem as outlined in other chapters.

ALLOCATING TAX DOLLARS TO SUPPORT EARLY-STAGE INNOVATION ECONOMY COMPANIES

Shifting from policies, the second category of how government can help innovation economy companies get started and grow would be to put some portion of those billions being allocated toward the bucket of economic development.

RESOURCE ALLOCATION: RESOURCE BOUNDARY CROSSING ECOSYSTEM BUILDING

No matter how much I might rail about the money we throw away on "build it and they will come" and "business attrac-

18 "Entrepreneur Visa Sponsorship," Venture Development Center, http://vdc.umb.edu/entrepreneur-visa-sponsorship/.

tion" outlined in chapter 3, I'm not naive enough to think these practices will be slowing down anytime soon. There are simply too many forces at work pushing dollars in those directions, including political realities that go beyond the themes touched on in this chapter.

But I'll still bring up the "Why are we trying to pick winners?" argument when I am speaking with politicians, including pointing out the fallacies behind thinking government can do a better job picking companies to invest in than the private sector can. Most startups will fail, yet a private investor will be happy with the positive return on the overall portfolio (just a few big wins more than cover all the losses). On the other hand, each publicly funded startup that goes bust creates a media event harmful to the politicians who were crowing at the time of the initial funding.

I advocate putting more public resources toward experimenting with programs described in this book that are aimed at fostering connectivity among entrepreneurs in the innovation economy and the resources they need to be successful, including those outside the entrepreneur's local community and institutions they might be affiliated with.

New programs lacking a proven-outcomes model will have risk. Some of that risk can be mitigated by ensuring there is a defined path to how the program will be advancing toward sustainability without relying on ongoing taxpayer support. Even better are programs already engaging private-sector investment from the outset, as that becomes a validation point in securing nongovernmental expertise as well as the intent of nurturing a new program in the direction of being self-sustaining.

As public resources get devoted to ecosystem-building programs, it is also important to seek out opportunities that help bust out of geographical and institutional boundaries that funding mechanisms can unwittingly create.

For example, restricting program access to entrepreneurs who reside in select ZIP codes means we're going to lose the opportunity to work with those in the next community over. Public funding is often given to recipient organizations with unnecessarily rigid constituent definitions that cause these organizations to start taking on a zero-sum-game outlook, as they won't go looking for others outside their defined boundaries, even when collaboration with other resources could bring mutual benefit.

RESOURCE ALLOCATION: RESEARCH INNOVATION ECONOMY AND COMMIT TO ECONOMIC DEVELOPMENT TRANSPARENCY

Another needed and appropriate use of public support would be data collection to help both government and the public better grasp the transformational change that is underway, illustrating that innovation lies at the base of where our economic future is headed.

Some people evolve their thinking about innovation economy startups after stumbling into a friend, relative, or colleague sharing an example of a young company growing from nothing to a major employer in a much shorter time period than traditional businesses.

But since local media doesn't cover startups, and most baby boomers just aren't plugged into the sources that show what's going on in the local innovation scene, government's role in sourcing and sharing relevant data can help drive awareness about trends that most people just aren't tuned into yet.

If a state government or academic researchers were to embrace the value that innovation economy growth has on overall job creation, it would be great to see a definition emerge that codifies who fits within this bucket of innovation economy companies, that others could begin adopting for reporting purposes. Just think about how much better we could make decisions on public policy, resource allocation, and even private investment if we were to know more precisely things like:

- Where are innovation economy companies located?
- What are their hiring, job growth, and salary trends?
- What industry subsegments are thriving?
- Where are entrepreneurs transitioning from college campuses to start new innovation economy companies?
- What are the Retainment and Magnet Quotients (described in chapter 2) for cities with populations greater than one hundred thousand people?
- How much angel investment is going into innovation economy companies?
- When and where are exit events happening and what contributed to these successes?

As many of the items from our wish list won't be easily teased out of existing government datasets, more inquiry will likely have to be conducted first, through funded research. Only after such research points to outcomes useful for policy and resource allocation will there be any effort to refine existing government data-collection methodology to capture relevant innovation economy trends on a broader scale.

But every state and local government has the opportunity to increase transparency around how economic development dollars being spent have defined targeted outcomes that are then tracked and reported to compare the actual results achieved against the original projections.

Ultimately, we believe the key metric for economic development should be framed around the number of taxpayer dollars spent per job created, both for an individual project being funded and in aggregated reporting at each level flowing up into the overall municipal and state budgets.

The cost-per-job metric is never mentioned when the project is announced, nor can we as taxpayers find out if the project actually delivered its intended job creation unless it blows up as a big miss and is then brought to light by what few remaining media sources out there are devoting resources to this kind of inquiry effort.

Businesses put big resources into tracking progress and comparing actual results against goals. It is a basic tenet that what gets measured can be managed. Given the billions being spent on economic development, just beefing up the resources to bring out transparency will not only permit better management, but also allow taxpayers to gauge both effectiveness of these programs and stewardship by the leaders we entrust to use our tax dollars wisely.

USING THE POWER TO CONVENE

Had I been elected to Congress, I knew of the inherent limitations to drive major policy change as a newbie in the 435-member House of Representatives. But while I would have absolutely worked toward smart job-growth policies, through-out my campaign I spoke frequently about my intent to leverage the congressional office's power to convene the right people as an important tool to drive change.

Suppose a path emerged where I believed collaboration among a bunch of independent organizations had potential to produce a positive change in the job-creating environment. An example I talked about would be the higher education community since there are a dozen colleges in New York's 22nd congressional district. As a congressman, I would have the opportunity to actually convene a meeting of those college presidents. With the right preparation and messaging, it would have been possi-ble to forge a collaborative path in leveraging college resources for job creation that would not have otherwise had a chance to come together.

The power to convene is not limited to gathering heads of organizations; it's also convincing highly influential people, described in chapter 6, to come together, especially people who are the doers getting things done in the community and have the give first approach so important to building change on a path others don't yet understand.

Tony Picente, our Oneida County executive, put this "conven-ing of doers" approach into play in helping us build support for a very nontraditional jobs-creation initiative we pro-posed to launch in Utica, New York, with help from Coeur d'Alene, Idaho–based Innovation Collective (visit Innovation Collective.co).

Innovation Collective built an impressive innovation commu-nity, going from near zero on the technology recognition scale to a place where Coeur d'Alene is now buzzing with startup knowledge and excitement. The community chose to embrace robotics as a focus—now producing innovations, churning out new companies, and attracting large corporations to come in and collaborate in the community. To do so in just a five-year sprint is faster progress than I've seen anywhere else in the country.

But even with an impressive model to leverage, there are a lot of obstacles to building support for a new economic vision presented by outsiders when you're in an Upstate town of sixty thousand people looking at empty, hulking manufacturing buildings and employment driven totally by local service, government, and nonprofits. Undeniably a Talent Exporting City.

We first got a few of the most highly influential people warmed up to the Innovation Collective approach, including bringing a delegation to Coeur d'Alene so they could see for themselves the substance behind the disciplined and creative approaches Innovation Collective took in engaging people from all segments of the community to participate in growing the innovation ethos.

As we shared that experience with Tony, his enthusiasm for supporting the initiative led to his convening a larger group of carefully selected HIPs who had the right profile as doers and give first people. Twenty-five of those HIPs came to the scheduled meeting despite less than two weeks' advance notice and Tony's purposely vague invitation about a job-creation initiative.

Over the course of a two-hour meeting, the Innovation Collective team presented a compelling story, bringing their experience to life. Then HIPs provided testimony of what they experienced from their visit to Coeur d'Alene and participation in Innovation Collective's annual Big Event conference. Receptivity proved to be so positive that seeds for building the local coalition immediately took root and collaboration involving multiple organizations and individuals began as we embarked on launching the Innovation Collective program with a multiyear commitment.

It will take years to prove out whether the initiative succeeds, but the launch was no doubt made possible because of a public official's adroit use of the power to convene, bringing the right people into the room and showing his personal support for an initiative that conventional thinking would conclude was nothing like the accepted ways of how we go about creating jobs.

APPLYING MORE GOOD JOBS PRINCIPLES IN ADVOCATING POLICY AND GOVERNMENT ACTION

Up to now, this chapter has presented policy and resource allocation suggestions that would appear to be more the domain of our public officials. Since most everyone reading this probably has roles falling outside of public office, let's segue to what we can do as individuals to help our officials get these messages.

First and foremost would be to recognize that changing the way government works is an even longer game than trying to help build an innovation economy in your community! That's why the bulk of this book has been concentrating on that which we can best control across the range of potential stakeholders in the prior four chapters.

But long game notwithstanding, government is still an effort worth putting a slice of energy toward. If we don't do it, who will?

We can also follow many of the same themes we've talked about in prior chapters. For example, we can apply the approaches on how to identify and cultivate relationships with highly influential people (chapter 6) as we look to engage officials who can help us.

In meeting with public officials, we want to avoid coming in to preach our point of view and then leave expecting we have shared some great insight that will prompt an official to take action.

Instead, we begin by getting to know the official well enough to understand their current view on job creation and what they would like to see done differently. Before going in depth on our advocacy agenda, better to have several questions ready that might weave in innovation economy themes so we can figure out the official's current knowledge and, more importantly, their interest and receptivity to these themes.

And by sticking to our principle of give first, we should hold back on the urge we might feel to present them with an ask on our first meeting and instead figure out ways we can help the official.

Based on the flow of discussion, we might uncover other ways we can help them, such as introducing a colleague or other resource aligned with the official's current needs. If we've advanced our relationship-building with other stakeholders in our community (chapter 6), investors (chapter 7), higher ed (chapter 8), or nonprofits (chapter 9), we probably have some relationship capital that can be productively deployed to help the official.

Never forget that officials holding elected office look at every interaction through the lens of "How will this help me get votes? Even if I believe it, do I have what I need to comfortably articulate it to others?"

My experience over many such interactions has taught me that, even though almost all public officials care about job creation, a surprising number fall into the trap of concluding they have the answers from what's been done in the past with "manage from the top" approaches as outlined in chapter 3. In such a scenario, it's a game-time decision on where to go with the discussion—is it worth more relationship-development energy or should we be moving on to find another official who might be more inclined to be receptive?

So I don't expect to advance an official's interest until they've first asked me enough questions that truly demonstrate their receptivity to a particular theme we've talked about. And most critically, I never expect to influence an official's outlook, much less behavior, with just a meeting or two. Relationships are formed based on multiple interactions that include my giving first without asking for something in return.

For the public official who does start to articulate the message, I consider opportunities to help them with things such as:

- Getting them speaking engagements before our innovation economy audiences, then equipping the official with messaging points to make those appearances valuable for both the audience and the official.

- Linking up the official to other like-minded peers in a legislative body. At county, state, and federal levels, the number of legislators can make it hard for them to find their tribe on this topic.
- Offer to be a resource in helping them evaluate the jobs impact of policy or allocation proposals coming before them or thinking about initiating. Finding out which committees they serve on may help target whom to approach and also which proposals going before that committee to monitor so we can step in proactively with input.
- Supporting their election or reelection with campaign contributions. I don't count on money buying votes, but I can assure you that contributions will generally earn access to open up a dialogue, as we've demonstrated we're committed supporters.
- Giving of our time to help in an official's election campaign. This is increasingly becoming the biggest need that officials have. Putting time and reputation on the line will mean even more than financial contributions.

VOICES FROM A COLLECTIVE HAVE MORE INFLUENCE

Long before I started on this journey to create jobs and build stronger communities, I was heavily engaged in advocacy for the industry of professional employer organizations. From TriNet's earliest days right up until I stepped down as CEO twenty years later, PEOs were in a constant struggle with state and federal public policy officials who had potential to regulate our nascent industry out of existence.

When TriNet started, there were perhaps only a dozen PEOs in the entire country. Given the high stakes and dearth of resources to advocate policy, it was against all odds that we were able to prevail on actually influencing legislation that today codify PEO licensing or compliance requirements across thirty-five states and the federal tax code (visit NAPEO.org).

That long journey drilled home for me the value of having a coordinated, collective effort staying focused on longer-term goals while steadily building a resource network to advance the advocacy process—including the relationship-development approaches noted in the prior section.

When an industry association has a shared economic interest from its members (as we did for PEOs), that's often a basis for forming a collective public advocacy effort. The problem for today's challenge of advocating change toward smart policy and resource allocation for jobs is that there is no association or convening entity to build a collective movement representing the interests of innovation economy entrepreneurs and communities wanting to shift from being Talent Exporting Cities to being more embracing of the next-generation startup companies.

So finding like-minded people who might be brought together for a collective effort is a central theme of what this book has been about. Applying this model for policy and government probably isn't going to be under the umbrella of a formal organization to start, but rather will be part of building a network and communications flow for those who pop up showing the interest.

It's not likely we'll see lots of startup entrepreneurs jumping aboard, as they're maniacally focused on trying to get their businesses beyond the survival stage. More seasoned entrepreneurs may have advantage in getting top-level access (especially if they're already recognized in their community), but they have other reasons keeping them on the sidelines. The more successful an entrepreneur is, the richer the palette of choices available to them.

Besides opportunity costs for their time, successful business-people think about risks ranging from the perceived conflicts of mixing business and politics and the frustratingly slow pace of any government process to concerns over what they want their name attached to. Who wants to spend so much energy and not see a result from doing so? This is the polar opposite of how action-oriented entrepreneurs who want to see them-selves as harbingers of change might lead.

So while I'm not counting on seeing large collective efforts emerge for the purpose of supporting cities embracing these innovation economy themes, I'll continue to be vigilant for new organizations popping up to build support such as we're doing with both Upstate Venture Connect and the Upstate Jobs Party.

A couple of other movements whose aims include policy advo-cacy are America's New Business Plan (visit StartUsUpNow. org) and the Center for American Entrepreneurship (visit StartupsUSA.org).

A promising development I'll be keeping an eye on is a 501(c) (3) nonprofit launched by Victor Hwang, former vice presi-dent for entrepreneurship at the Kauffman Foundation and author of *Rainforest: Secrets to Growing the Next Silicon Valley*, mentioned in chapter 7. Right to Start aims to champion our entrepreneurs and communities to drive awareness and inspire change at both grasstops and grassroots levels, includ-ing activating individuals to become engaged in advocating for public policy changes and community ecosystem-building (visit RightToStart.org).

The MoreGoodJobs.org website includes an access path to our More Good Jobs community site where you'll find a policy section inviting everyone to report what we're seeing so we can all be better informed about collectives emerging outside our own view. Register on the site and engage with others on this job-creating journey.

SUMMARY

- Government doesn't create jobs—entrepreneurs do. But public policy and government administration can be factors shaping the environment in which job creators can be thwarted or have their potential unleashed.
- Government can create policies that support growth of Magnet Cities by approving tax incentives to invest in startups, restricting noncompete agreements, and encouraging skilled immigration.
- Government can allocate resources to cross-boundary ecosystem-building and researching the innovation economy to guide our future decisions.
- Bringing about change in government is needed but requires a long-term commitment in building one relationship at a time.
- We can influence people in government by applying many of the same approaches of developing relationships with highly influential people, including give first.
- Given the absence of organizations out there with a mission of advocating public-policy support for job-creating entrepreneurs, it's important to look for opportunities to build a collective voice on these issues.

CHAPTER 11

ARE WE READY TO LEAD CHANGE?

Never doubt that a small group of thoughtful,
committed citizens can change the world;
indeed, it's the only thing that ever has.

—MARGARET MEAD

We've spent the past chapters looking at potential stakeholders in our community that could join us—highly influential people, private seed capital investors, higher education, nonprofits, and government—and what they can do to support an effort to create more innovation economy companies, and thus more jobs, in our communities.

Each of these stakeholders has a potential part to play in this change, but throughout these discussions, I've tried to point out that they are resources to be tapped more than they are the initiating force that will actually drive change.

While I'm certain we'll continue to see some top-down, government-driven initiatives, after a decade of tinkering on this journey, I have yet to see a single example I can point to where a government-led initiative has actually worked as the driving catalyst fostering an ecosystem of innovation economy companies growing out of the challenging circumstances found in a Talent Exporting City.

If we look deeply into how the Magnet Cities found their legs, the forces of culture and the impact of a few farsighted business leaders who collaborated in shaping a connected environment had so much more to do with how today's hotbeds of startups evolved.

Since you've shown enough interest in the topic to arrive at this late stage of the book, the question now becomes whether this is just an interesting intellectual exercise or the beginning of your own journey to step into the fray helping drive change yourself?

Before we get to thinking through any personal action plan, our journey has to begin with self-assessment about what our own motivations might be to dedicate time to something that won't show measurable impact, even over a few years.

IS HELPING TO CREATE MORE GOOD JOBS RIGHT FOR ME?

Maybe you've already achieved some professional success and you're asking yourself what's next. Maybe you're looking to put your talents to use to have the largest possible impact on the most people. Maybe you're a seasoned entrepreneur exiting from your company and looking beyond the path of just starting another company. For whatever reason, maybe you're looking for a fresh challenge with something that excites you.

In my case, it was a combination of these things. In Bo Burlingham's excellent book *Finish Big*, he profiles entrepreneurs who have successfully exited their companies, some for billions of dollars. While some of the profiled exited entrepreneurs are extremely happy, a surprising number are unfulfilled. My interactions with Bo as he was writing *Finish Big* helped clarify some of my own thinking around why I was so deliberate in making the choices I did to avoid squandering my time and resources after stepping down as chairman and having TriNet go public.

I was fortunate to have latitude to put my attention wherever I liked, and this mission to change a regional economy by creating more good jobs called me. Not only did it have potential to make a real impact on the lives of many people, but I knew I'd get more fulfillment and joy in the process than were I to restart the entrepreneurial journey by launching another company.

But even today, ten years after starting, some would call our ecosystem outcomes in Upstate New York still uncertain. It's too difficult to actually measure the number of jobs attributable to our direct intervention. Therein lies the crux of the problem, going to the heart of anyone's self-assessment: people ask themselves "If I can't get credit for something, is it worth doing?"

If you believe that being personally acknowledged as the changemaker is the reason to become involved, then pursuing more good jobs is not the right journey for you. Not only because it will be too hard to measure the actual impact of connections you foster, but the underlying motivation of pursuing recognition is contrary to the very principle of give first.

Similarly, if you are a service provider in the community, envisioning the potential of how a thriving startup ecosystem could help your own business grow, this journey may not be right for you. While it's true that more startups could present more opportunities for your business, I can tell you that other people will be very quick to sniff out your motives if you are being driven by a commercial imperative, and you'll be sidelined from getting help from the people you want to engage. It's true that eventual recognition or commercial opportunities might flow your way, but that can't be the primary basis to become involved.

Give first means giving without any expectation of getting a return, other than our belief that what we're doing is helping another person and is also the right thing for the community. Good things are almost certainly going to happen as we make progress; we just can't predict where, when, how, or with whom that will come about.

So if I were to summarize motivations that made sense for me to become involved beyond the starting point of a passion to the mission of helping others create companies and jobs, it would be things such as:

- Liking the idea of taking on a challenge so big others think it is not possible to make a difference.
- Leveraging the knowledge, skills, and relationships I have to make the greatest possible impact on others.
- Pleasure that comes with hanging out with a bunch of like-minded people who are committing to the same difficult cause—this is how true bonds are formed.
- Being forced into staying abreast of new technologies and developments, a necessity to be relevant in almost every personal interaction, so I've got to keep consuming new content and observing changes and trends that too many

others in my generation are not even close to seeing until after they've happened.

- Believing that sticking to the path we're on will lead to good things happening, even if the outcome measures are a bit fungible as we rely on anecdotal evidence more than government-reported stats on overall job creation.

If you think about it, these five motivations are similar to common reasons someone launches a startup. It's not a coincidence that people with a background in at least one entrepreneurial gig have some relevant DNA that can also have the biggest impact in getting others engaged.

GATHERING INTEL ON THE LOCAL STARTUP SCENE

Let's say you've proceeded through the self-assessment phase and found enough reasons to start on your own journey to become involved. It's probably best to start with a community scan to find what things are currently going on for others helping startups.

Events are a great way to open up dialogue and meet people through creative collisions. If you're a newbie, it may take some effort to find the groups out there where people are meeting. Ask around, including any startup company founders you might find by talking with service providers (accountants, lawyers, consultants, and others who might have startup customers), as well as your friends, local economic development organizations, colleges, chambers of commerce, local business organizations, etc.

If you're early in your career or think that going into events where you don't know anyone sounds a bit scary, then I strongly recommend checking out the previously mentioned *Meet 100 People* by Pat Hedley. It's a great resource, packed with insight and practical tips on how to go about finding and developing relationships with people you don't yet know (visit and purchase from Meet100People.com).

I've attended events where the organization's mission or event format didn't click with me, but I would still go through a few exposures if the people attending included others in the community involved in innovation economy companies. Colliding with someone at one meeting has many times resulted in sparking a connection that helped me forge a relationship path outside of the event where the initial collision occurred.

INTENTION BECOMES CLEAR WITH ACTION

Having good intentions that others don't understand can actually result in some skepticism. As we meet others at an event, people are naturally curious about why we're there. As the events are broadly tied to business, you are likely to get probing questions from folks wondering, "What's your angle?"

This was definitely the case when I first stepped down from my chairman role at TriNet to begin this effort with UVC. I was a bit out of circulation since I'd spent the prior decade commuting between Little Falls and Silicon Valley, and all my Little Falls time was spent with family. I had no network to speak of in Upstate New York at that time. I began to seek out and attend meetups and any gathering I could find that involved people interested in startups and innovation economy topics.

Even without any ulterior motives beyond learning and looking for opportunities to give, I encountered some of that skepticism myself. My credentials weren't understood or appreciated. When I described what we were seeking to do in starting Upstate Venture Connect as a new nonprofit, the common refrain I heard was that it would never last. Helping entrepreneurs get connected to resources? What does that mean? It simply didn't compute for most people because it didn't fit the conventional model of economic development.

But I kept showing up at the various gatherings that had startup people coming together. I can't overemphasize the value of repeated exposure to the same group, especially in a place where boundary-crossing collaboration and open ideas might not yet be the norm. It was only through repeated exposure, month after month and eventually year after year, that the skeptics began to see that I wasn't going to give up. And as I figured out ways in which I could help them, while asking for nothing in return, more of the skeptics slowly began the conversion process to embrace the ethos of give first and eventually become supporters of UVC.

CHANGE HAPPENS WHEN LEADERS EMERGE

Nothing of significance in this world happens without leaders. From world-changing political movements like the American Revolution to incredible businesses like Apple or Amazon, every movement starts with leaders who are willing to take a stand and get others involved. Any major change is a group effort, and every group effort begins with someone who is able to galvanize and engage other leaders to support each other in accomplishing a hard goal.

In our effort to create more good jobs in our country, and especially in the effort to create more successful businesses with a high job multiplier, few communities have someone intentionally leading that charge. Without clear leaders dedicated to that mission, it's hard to envision a successful path to reach the outcome that we're seeking.

It's tempting to think that those leaders in public office, economic development, academia, or even corporate roles will lead this charge. But they can be entrenched in systems with their own incentives and motivations. The ideal leaders don't take charge because it's their job description or because they are a part of an organization that requires it. The leaders needed to make things happen in Talent Exporting Cities will take charge because they are intrinsically motivated to bring about the change we're talking about.

For many who get involved in a mission like this—especially young people—leadership can be scary. Those who don't have experience leading often perceive leadership as a magical set of skills that must be mastered before they can have an effect. This isn't the case at all. Leadership is simply taking action and finding or guiding like-minded others to collaborate toward a common goal.

WHAT ARE THE TRAITS OF A GREAT LEADER?

There are tens of thousands of leadership books on the market today, so the last thing you need is to be inundated with more generic leadership advice. However, there are attributes that are particularly important in leading the kind of movement we're speaking about. I will discuss them briefly here as perhaps a self-assessment tool to figure out if this is a journey that aligns with your own values.

CREDIBILITY

We want to be credible in all of our relationships, but this is the one attribute, above all others, that is essential for leadership. To me, credibility begins with integrity: doing the right thing, as so many of our choices can have underpinnings on ethical and moral grounds. But integrity for me also means doing what I say I am going to do. Or, more specifically, delivering on the commitments I make to other people.

We all have that intention to deliver on our commitments, yet the more things we get involved with, the greater the number of people we're making commitments to. Even at early stages in our career, when we have fewer activities and organizational connections, it is easy to be caught in the circumstance of having told someone we were going to do something that we just let slip through the cracks and never get around to.

People respect leaders who simply deliver on the promises they make. Not just the big, public commitments but the little things that are just one person's word to another. As I think about why others chose to follow me across rebel leadership pursuits I've been on, I would put this attribute of keeping my word on even the small things as the foundation for having been able to engage others.

CONNECTOR

At its core, leadership involves connecting people. It's about bringing people and resources together to help everyone achieve their goals. This isn't an inborn trait or something you either have or you don't. I believe that applying constant effort and attention to understanding the needs of people I meet, the opportunities for how I can help by connecting one person to another always seem to emerge.

The biggest, most important part of being a connector building a movement is to do so by giving first. I don't think about my endgame or what I want from someone as I meet them. Instead, as I ask questions to understand the goals of the individual I'm interacting with, once I see any alignment for the cause and potential to contribute, then my mind just starts to click into "Who or what do I know that could possibly help this person?"

Depending on the circumstances, if I see the fit, I might make a referral connection to someone I just met right on the spot, especially if it can be to another person in the same room. Or it might come later. If I've asked the right questions to understand whom I'm interacting with, I've uncovered a few things of possible interest that I'll then be thinking about and perhaps note in my contact record for them.

What's really cool is when I run across another person who also starts asking me the same kind of discovery questions—I can see we are both in a connector mindset. That's when I know that I've just found a new friendship that is likely to evolve into a burgeoning relationship. I am going to work extra hard to find ways to help that person, since they can be a highly valued resource as part of the leadership circle we need to grow the movement.

As the scope of our movement grows, we may need to become more systematic in our connections. I use a CRM system to track contacts by categories, skills, and needs, and add notes each time I speak with them to remember things like their spouse's name, their hobbies, and any major life events they have coming up.

You can use those connections to create an email list—with their permission, of course. UVC sends out newsletters and has an active stream across multiple social media platforms. All of this helps to share relevant information and connection opportunities with people in our network who are working toward our mission of creating an innovation economy across Upstate New York.

HUMILITY

Especially important in this kind of movement is humility. Its opposite is arrogance, and who wants to follow an arrogant leader?

There's no doubt I find myself out of my depth sometimes. After almost a decade working on this problem, it would be easy to slip into the mindset of feeling like I have solutions that just need to be spouted out when I run into a knowledgeable and sophisticated person who doesn't yet understand they're living in a Talent Exporting City, or the opportunities brought about by having more innovation economy companies as opposed to manufacturing.

My pontificating on that wouldn't be the right path to win a new friend. Nor would my using valuable airtime extolling my Silicon Valley journey. I've only come to recognize the vastness of what I don't know. As leaders, our job isn't to have all the answers—it's to bring together the people who have the answers and move them toward meaningful progress.

To do this requires humility. Understand that we don't know everything and have the confidence to trust others along the journey. If we find ourselves doing more talking than listening, it's probably a clue that we're putting too much energy into showing what we know as opposed to learning from others.

WALK IN SOMEONE ELSE'S SHOES

The final leadership trait I'd like to discuss is one that I don't see mentioned in many leadership books, but that I consider one of the attributes that has helped me the most in my building support with other people: the ability to put myself in other people's shoes.

Early in my career, I was lucky enough to live overseas in two very different cultures—first in Japan, and subsequently in southern Italy. These experiences shocked my system, as the norms and expectations in each culture were so different from what I'd grown up expecting in America, as well as so different from each other. If there are two opposite cultures in the world, they are found in Japan and southern Italy.

In both countries I worked with trade unions. In order for me to do my job well, I had to understand and empathize with their points of view, which were completely different from my own. To work with them cooperatively, I needed to understand deeply how they saw the world. I learned very quickly to see things from other people's perspective.

By the time I came back to the United States and started TriNet, I had developed a heightened sensitivity to trying to figure out other people's perspectives. I was so much better equipped to put myself in the shoes of people I was interacting with. This was especially beneficial in sales and allowed me to find success bringing all of TriNet's sales over the company's first six years, even though I lacked prior sales experience. Later, these same skills continued to serve me as I grew our team.

To succeed as a leader, we must understand people's thinking. Why might they say no to our request? What fears do they have? What truly matters to them, and how can what we're doing support that?

Leading people effectively all comes down to understanding other people's views, realizing they're different from ours, and letting other people know you hear them and care about them.

YOU'RE ALREADY A LEADER

Some people can be intimidated by leadership training, seeing leadership as a mountain they must climb before they are worthy of leading others.

That simply isn't true. You are already a leader in certain areas of your life—whether at home, among your friends, at church, or in other activities—and advice around leadership exists to help you expand this area and support people more deeply when you do lead them.

Don't overcomplicate leadership. The leadership training industry was designed to make you believe that you need it before you can lead, but that isn't how leadership works. As soon as you decide you want to accomplish something and find others who want to accomplish the same thing, you are a leader. Everything else is just how to do that more effectively.

PLAYING THE LONG GAME

None of this happens overnight. When I first started visiting other cities and going to events where nobody knew me or understood what I was trying to do, I wasn't any kind of a leader in the community.

By applying the ideas in this chapter, showing up consistently, and giving first, I've been able to develop a deep and productive set of relationships across a broadly dispersed region. Today, Upstate Venture Connect has a network of seventeen-thousand-plus people. Fast-growing companies are starting to sprout in the Upstate community, including billion-dollar businesses like CommerceHub, Datto, and ACV Auctions. And venture capital investments in the region are at an all-time high: Buffalo companies raised $250 million in 2019, with the rest of the region not far behind. These and other observations reflecting what we've seen evolve over our decade of putting these principles in play are profiled in my partner Nasir's post at UVC.org/reflections.

It's important to accept that leadership is a long-term game. There's no finish line to reach, since the more we succeed, the larger our scope will become. We started with just a few relationships in a couple cities Upstate. As the collective grew, we shifted from being the only ones talking about these themes to ever-widening the circle so we were coordinating the efforts of a distributed group of local leaders who share our passion for advancing this mission.

This book represents a further step in this journey. Rather than focusing on my own region, my goal is to unlock more people to become leaders (and, eventually, leaders of leaders too). There is unlimited work to be done. Our job is to facilitate the focus of smart people to move toward these goals, so that we can create the types of communities that flourish, filled with good jobs.

Taking these same principles and applying them in impoverished countries is the goal of our nonprofit Entrepreneurs Across Borders. Starting with our pilot in the Caribbean, our goal is to prove out a scalable model that connects emerging entrepreneurs to the people and resources that can help transform lives and communities (visit EABorders.org).

None of this will happen quickly, but what fun would it be if it did?

In truth, I'm probably not going to live long enough to see the full impact of these efforts play out in the communities I am involved with. Neither may you in your community. There's something beautiful and amazing about that. The point isn't for us to reach an end-state, it's to move toward an ideal and make people better off along the way.

At times, while the challenge can feel enormous, I know the outcome is worth the effort. We don't have to feel like Don Quixote tilting at windmills. This is a journey, and that journey is in itself a reward.

SUMMARY

- This journey isn't right for everyone. But if you are looking for a challenge that will make an impact, build a community, and stretch you, this may be for you.
- Leadership can be intimidating, but it isn't magic. Leadership is simply taking action and engaging and guiding others to take the actions needed to work toward a common goal.
- To become great leaders, we should focus on building credibility by doing what we say we are going to do, showing up and giving first, connecting people, staying humble, and putting ourselves in other people's shoes.
- This is a long journey, and a leader's job is to help engage the right people with a long-term perspective so that our community can stay the course.

CONCLUSION

THE REWARD IS THE JOURNEY

There is no limit to what a man can do or where he can go if he doesn't mind who gets the credit.
—A PLAQUE RONALD REAGAN KEPT ON
HIS DESK IN THE WHITE HOUSE

I'm the son of a factory worker.

I grew up with my dad working in an environment where "management" meant running roughshod over the workers on the assembly floor. That unjust balance of power is what led to the rise of trade unions, which began shifting influence from those with capital toward organized labor. Hearing about how that evolved over my dad's work life helped me understand the importance of how someone's work impacts their overall life. That's what caused me to select human resources as my major while still early in my college studies.

Since then, that's what my whole life has been focused on: figuring out paths for how companies can do better in supporting their workers. At my deepest level, I believe in the importance of how jobs and work end up impacting families and communities. It's why I worked in human resources, it's why I started TriNet, and it's why I do what I do today.

I believe many entrepreneurs are on a similar journey. They may not see the path yet—as Steve Jobs said, we can only connect the dots looking backwards—but many of us do what we do in the service of a deeper mission.

The challenge, counterintuitively, comes when our needs are met. At some point, many entrepreneurs reach a stage where they are comfortable. They've achieved some professional success, their family is stable, and they don't need more money. And yet, too many of us default to starting the next company. I don't believe it's because we're greedy or want more zeroes on our bank balance. Rather, it's because starting another company is natural for us.

In a strange way, despite how ridiculously challenging starting a company is, I realized that for me, starting a company would have been the easy way out. I needed to go beyond what I'd already proven in business and try my hand at something new and personally challenging. More importantly, I wanted to do work that I believed in enough to think: *I'm doing what I was born to be doing. It just took a whole lot of other things first before I could get started.*

Too often, when people become successful, they make a shift where they pull everything in and avoid taking risks—professionally, financially, or reputationally. But where's the fun in life if you can't take some risks?

The truth is this: we all know our days on this planet are limited. It's not fun to think about, but it's reality. We only have a set amount of time here, and the biggest decisions we make in our life are how we want to spend that precious nonrenewable resource.

It can be scary to step into the unknown and pursue the improbable. Despite my prior business success, as I began this journey, I spent a lot of time thinking about the fact that I'm only one man. What could I possibly do as a single person to help unleash the potential in my community? How could I not only create good-paying jobs, but lift the economic opportunities for people struggling with disadvantages as they sought to improve their lives?

Back in 1979, when being an entrepreneur wasn't as in vogue as it is today, Bernie Goldhirsh founded *Inc.* magazine and proclaimed that for entrepreneurs, "business is the canvas." His point was that entrepreneurs are not only crazy enough to think we can make what's never been made before, but we're also creative enough to make it happen.

Bernie was right. In the years since then, more and more entrepreneurs have dreamed big and accomplished world-changing things, their businesses acting as the canvas for their creativity and imagination.

If you're an entrepreneur, you made that leap as you built your business, and I'm hoping you'll consider making that leap again. Except, rather than using a canvas you're familiar with, experiment with a new one. For leaders in potential innovation economy hubs, your community is the canvas.

YOUR COMMUNITY NEEDS YOU

I don't have any grand plan for my legacy. I have no idea if any of the things I've started will stand the test of time to live beyond me. Some people want buildings with their name on them; some people want statues or some other monument to their greatness.

That's not what I want. For me, it's not about celebrity or even permanency. It's about having made a difference somewhere along the way.

What matters is whether I have helped others be inspired enough to act. If people remember me as someone who got a few others closer to a mission they believed in—perhaps helping build a robust community of people who bring value to the world—I'm happy with that. I don't need or expect any recognition.

We are living at an incredible time in history. There are fewer barriers to entrepreneurship than ever, and more potential for fulfilling, meaningful, highly paid work than at any other time in history. But because we are in a transition into a new economy, many communities aren't reaping the benefits of these amazing changes.

If you feel, as I do, that this is a problem you'd like to contribute to solving, now is your chance to do so. You have the roadmap. You have the skills. All that's left is to take action.

Think about the unemployed families in your city. Think about the people working jobs they hate or moving across the country, away from their families, to find the work they want. These people's lives will transform if there are good jobs within your community.

Are you going to help make it possible to create more of them?

THE NEXT STEP

To join our community of leaders who want to engage in transforming their cities, please register on our website at MoreGoodJobs.org.

The website and its access to our More Good Jobs Community will together include valuable resources in helping to build a Magnet City, such as blog posts, discussion threads, reader polls, data based on our research team's findings, virtual office hours featuring various experts, and up-to-date public policy suggestions. We hope you'll join us.

All proceeds from the sale of this book will go toward the philanthropic commitment I make in supporting others who are growing their startup communities. We'll list grants made to related nonprofit organizations and invite grant requests to be submitted to our UpMobility Foundation (visit UpMobility. org).

Our joining together to share best practices and resources is an important pathway for helping each other transform our communities!

ACKNOWLEDGMENTS

Even with a clear vision of the desired outcome, as with any company or cause that gets traction, this book reached publication only because of a whole bunch of people whose collective support made the journey I've been on possible.

Scribe Media was referred to me by another entrepreneur friend who was working with them, since Scribe has a strong record in the space of business books from people who live the story as opposed to just imagining it.

Totally unanticipated was my good fortune with Scribe's co-founder, Zach Obront, taking enough personal interest in the concept and story to put it under his personal purview of author support and editor.

Zach's chops as an Austin-based entrepreneur were critical to understanding the issues facing early-stage companies as well as the viewpoint of a supportive local ecosystem. That, along with disciplined execution and a dedicated team, helped nurture me along as a newbie author to go through all the essential steps to get this book finished in a way we hope you found value in. From strategy to editing, production, and marketing, I can't say enough about how this team helped me take semi-plausible ideas and bad writing and evolved it to the finished product.

About a year before publication, we actually had a full draft ready to go, but I pushed back on it, as I felt it didn't have enough empirical evidence to shore up assertions I was making anecdotally.

That led to a long detour to find and engage a research team headed by Professors Brett Orzechowski of Utica College and Jason Kuruzovich of Rensselaer Polytechnic Institute, two incredibly talented academics who are also committed to building a startup ecosystem, not just with academic research, but rolling up their sleeves to help build community in their respective cities. Anuj Chauhan of RPI also provided valuable research support.

My Upstate Venture Connect co-founder and partner, Nasir Ali, was probably the single biggest influence for me to be committed for such an extended period. Nasir's intellect towers above mine, but it is his integrity and our shared vision of a long-term commitment that has made our synergistic partnership produce so much more than either of us could have done on our own.

UVC getting Kate Cartini to come aboard as our chief marketing officer was another critical building block, as she delivered the combination of marketing sophistication, technical savvy, uber-connection, and buy-in toward building a startup community that made it possible to scale up UVC's community of supporters across a broadly dispersed geography.

There are many sources of inspiration from a startup community perspective that also matter.

The individuals profiled in my description of Upstate New York's startup community are living examples of how shared values and commitment are making the difference in forging change for the benefit of our entire region.

Brad Feld sets standards for give first and accelerating startup communities, which, no matter how hard I pedal toward, I don't ever expect to measure up to. Personal interactions with authors and entrepreneur advocates Jim Collins, Victor Hwang, Bo Burlingham, Verne Harnish, Mario Morino, and Keith Alper have broadened my perspective and shaped ideas that led to these pages.

My longtime personal assistant Mary Lou Herringshaw keeps the trains running and commitments fulfilled across an ever-growing set of relationships and new entities created, which now contribute to both job-growing and community-building endeavors.

Of course, none of this would have been possible had I not been through TriNet's Silicon Valley experience so integral to my outlook today. The number of colleagues who made that possible are too numerous to mention. Most of Team TriNet recognize that my partnering with Doug Devlin, who began as my next-door neighbor and evolved to become my partner, CFO, and COO, was the single most important relationship for building the company. Jack Stack, founder of SRC and co-author of *The Great Game of Business*, was the inspiration and brains behind how Doug and I learned to lay the foundation for the culture of employee ownership that made TriNet's growth possible and still thrives today under my successor, Burton Goldfield's, leadership.

But all of TriNet's growth was preceded by the contributions of the late Dr. T. Joe Willey, father of the PEO industry, who, like my wife Krista and my dad, believed in me when few others understood or appreciated what we were working toward, much less the reward in that journey, no matter how improbable.

I stand on the shoulders of giants and am a very lucky man.

ABOUT THE AUTHOR

MARTIN BABINEC founded Silicon Valley-based TriNet in 1988, serving as CEO for the company's first twenty years and Chairman until 2010. TriNet's cloud-based HR services help more than 14,000 small to midsize companies, and the company has grown to annual sales of $4 billion and is listed on the NYSE.

In 1999, Babinec relocated his family from Silicon Valley to his hometown of Little Falls, New York, where he founded Upstate Venture Connect (a nonprofit dedicated to accelerating the growth of startups across Upstate New York), StartFast Ventures (a seed fund with an actively engaged network of entrepreneur mentors and investors), and UpVentures Capital (where he makes direct investments in startup companies and serves as a limited partner and advisor to a dozen venture capital and seed funds).

In 2016, Babinec founded the Upstate Jobs Party (UJP) and ran as an independent candidate in New York's 22nd Congressional District. Advocating policies and private-sector engagement to spur job growth, the race earned national recognition as the only congressional race in which an independent candidate was competitive. He continues to lead UJP on a path to earn constituted party status in New York State as a vehicle to influence political discourse in reversing regional population decline.

INDEX

Tables and figures are indicated by an italic *f* and *t* following the page number.

A

example of, 15–21

with innovation economy job generation, 56–57f, 58–62

predictions about, 44f–45, 56–57f, 58–62, 59t, 60t

with virtuous cycle of creating companies, 49–55, 62

cloud-based services, 52–53, 155

coaching model of education, 164, 173, 189–190, 217

coding courses, commercial, 189–190

Coeur d'Alene, ID, 221, 251–253

collective advocacy for public policies, 256–259

collective bargaining, 37–38

college alumni expatriates, recruitment of, 140–142

college graduates, relocation and retainment of, 19–20, 58–62, 59t, 60t, 185–187. *see also* higher education, connections with

Collins, Jim, 113

commitments, keeping, 269

communication

    in Cornell's eShip program, 204–205

    face-to-face dynamic for, 88, 147–148

    failure of New York State with, 242

    by UVC, 110, 118, 126, 146, 271, 283

    for visibility of positive cultural norms, 126, 127

    for visibility with HIPs, 146

community-based philanthropy, 218–221

community benefits of innovation economy, 29, 35, 40–47, 44f, 53–54

Community Catalyst award by UVC, 101

community change

    by changing culture (*see* culture change for innovation; leadership for community change)

    for entrepreneurs (*see* relationships in entrepreneurial communities)

    with improvement as explicit goal, 123–124, 226–228

    partners for (*see* partners for community building)

Community Foundation of Herkimer and Oneida Counties, 220–221

community foundations, 218–221

companies in innovation economy (startups)

    capital and guidance for (*see* early-stage private capital; investment for startups)

    cultures of, 113–114, 125

    defined, 30–31, 239

    exits of, 159–161, 173–174, 180–181

    failures of, 75, 173, 247

median income, changes in, 43–44*f,* 45, 47, 58–59

Meet 100 People (Hedley), 191, 266

meetings, government power to convene, 250–253

meetup format for events, 95, 118, 197–199

member-managed seed capital funds, 163. *see also* seed capital funds, member-managed

mentorship of new entrepreneurs, 75–76, 78–79, 144, 169–170, 175–176, 217

minorities in entrepreneurship, 79–80, 83, 105–109, 111, 222–223

mission-driven organizations, 226–229, 233

Mohawk Valley (Upstate New York), 13, 15–17, 51–52, 137, 208–209, 220–221

Mohawk Valley Community College (MVCC), 208–209

More Good Jobs Community website and resources, 259, 283

Moretti, Enrico, 36–38, 41, 55, 57

motivations for potential leaders, 262–265

multiplier effect in job creation, 36–44*f,* 47, 81

Musk, Elon, 49, 50, 72–73

N

Nashville, TN, 44*f,* 45, 57*f,* 59*t,* 62

National Foundation for American Policy (NFAP), 244

national or global markets, need for, 31, 37, 40, 42, 54

networks

    entrepreneurs' need for, 74–76, 78, 81–82, 191 (*see also* relationships in entrepreneurial communities)

    of HIPs, 79–80, 132–133

    for political advocacy, 256–259

New Geography of Jobs, The (Moretti), 36, 55

new ideas, creation of and openness to, 51, 65, 118–120, 127

new markets, creation of, 152, 154, 239

New York State, economic initiatives in, 69–71, 143, 241–242. *see also* Upstate New York

NextCorps, 216

noncompete agreements, restriction of, 242–243

nonprofits, benefits of community wealth for, 45, 220

nonprofits (NPs), partnering with, 213–233

    competitive vs. cooperative mindset and, 229–230

    economic development organizations for, 143, 216–218, 228

    with giving first attitude, 224–225

    importance of, 226–228, 233

Roc Growth, 139–140

Rochester, NY

public policy problems in, 67–74, 77

turnaround opportunities for, 81–83, 166–167, 187

tax base, increases of, 45

tax incentives, 20–21, 38–39, 69–71, 240–242

tax rates, low vs. high, 15, 237–238

Tech Garden, 214–215, 216

Techstars model, 121, 144, 174, 175

tech transfer process in higher education, 167–168, 199–203

Tesla, 72–73

Thiel, Peter, 50

thINCubator space, 209–210, 220–221

"Thoughts on Sourcing Black Companies and Entrepreneurs" (Feld), 106–109

top-down approaches to community change, 20–21, 45–46, 67–73

traditional businesses vs. innovation economy companies, 54–55, 63–64, 77, 90–93, 239

training of entrepreneurs

accelerator programs for, 143–144, 172–173, 175–177, 184

coaching for, 164, 173, 189–190, 217

mentorship for, 75–76, 78–79, 144, 169–170, 175–176, 217

social enterprises for, 221–223

transactional exchanges vs. giving first, 122, 136

transparency in economic development spending, 250

Trenchard, Bill, 141, 145

TriNet

company culture and success of, 113–114, 272–273

customer base for, 40, 64–66, 115

employees of, 32, 42–43

HR outsourcing as new idea by, 13–17, 91, 119, 277–278

PEO advocacy and, 256–257

support from entrepreneur community for, 14–18, 63–67, 75–76, 90–93, 120

Trump administration, 245

trust, sources and culture of, 89–90, 90–93

Tucson, AZ, 44f, 45, 57f, 59, 60t, 62

U

Ulrich, Bob, 92

universities. *see* higher education, connections with

university research-commercialization processes, 167–168, 199–203

UNY50 Leadership Network, 102, 171

CPSIA information can be obtained
at www.ICGtesting.com
Printed in the USA
LVHW110016291020
670141LV00012B/63/J

9 781544 508481